5067 Boxing Greats
Copyright ©1998 Quadrillion Publishing Ltd
Published in 1998 by Colour Library Direct, an imprint of
Quadrillion Publishing Ltd,
Godalming, Surrey, GU7 1XW, England

ISBN 1-85833-856-5

CREDITS

Project Editor
Chris Stone

Designer
Peter Laws

Copy-editor
Jillian Stewart

Production
Neil Randles, Ruth Arthur, Karen Staff

Director of Production
Graeme Procter

Colour reproduction
Global Colour, Malaysia

Printed and bound
Graficromo, S.A.

BOXING
GREATS

LEGENDARY BOXERS, FIGHTS AND MOMENTS

Steve Bunce

CONSULTANT EDITOR **BOB MEE**

Colour
Library
Direct

Contents

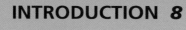

Foreword

▲ THE PRIDE OF THE YEMEN

Naseem Hamed is nothing short of a living legend in his home country of Yemen, where his achievements have been celebrated in this series of commemorative stamps.

The great fighters had moves. Muhammad Ali had sweet punches from hidden places, Willie Pep was slick and Sugar Ray Robinson could do it at all weights. Great fighters.

I want to be a great fighter, up there with the legends for history to remember forever. I know I can do it, I can fight five ways and I have a champion's heart. I showed that against Kevin Kelley.

In Boxing Greats the best fighters and the best fights are together in one volume. Not all of the fighters are as famous as Ali, Pep or Robinson, but they all deserve their place in this book.

The modern greats have their place also. Marvin Hagler, Sugar Ray Leonard and Roberto Duran. They were in some of the best fights ever.

There are great fighters now inlcuding Oscar De La Hoya, Roy Jones and myself. We are part of boxing history and we share the pages with all of the other fighters from boxing's past.

Boxing is part of a living tradition and tradition is important to me. I know you will find something new and different in this book; it will help you understand why boxing is such a great sport with a great history.

PRINCE NASEEM HAMED

Ancient PUGS *and* VICTORIAN GENTLEMEN

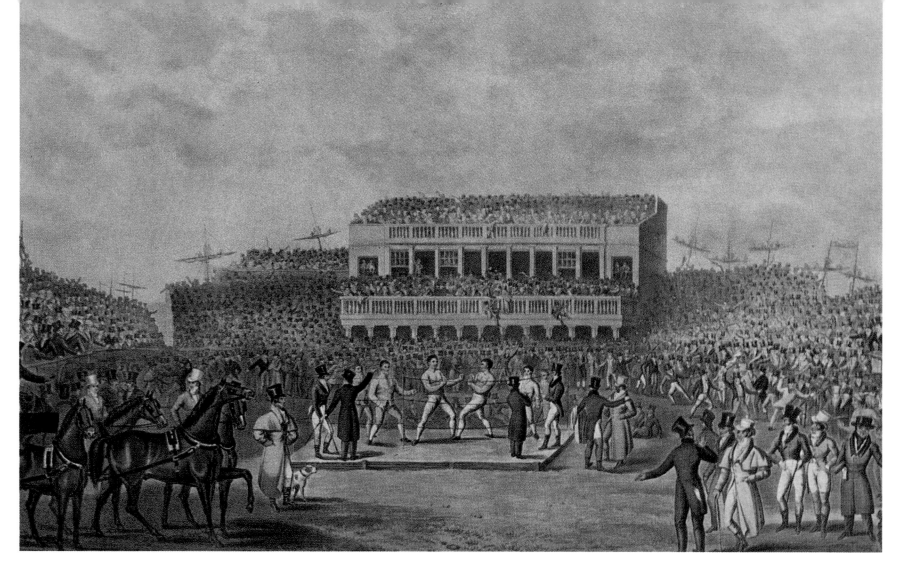

The top pugilists were in demand as the sport began to expand

The art of boxing was born at the Bear Gardens, by the River Thames in London, in the mid-17th century. The vulgar idols of the day, however, were not the pugilists, but fighting bears with names like Goldilocks, Rose of Bedlam and Mad Besse. The fist-fights took place on the same bill as the bear-baiting, in the sheds and scaffolds of London, but were considered a lesser attraction at the time.

In 1684, a so-called Boarded House, in fields near what is now Oxford Circus in central London, was used to bait bears, bulls and dogs. In 1719 the owner formed a partnership with James Figg and the Boarded House soon took on a new guise as an "entertainment" centre which boasted a wide variety of combat games. Figg was a touring swordsman who took advantage of his new base to explore the building's gore-stained past. He combined fist and sword with women, freaks and wild animals during a six-year reign of original spectator events. On Figg's stage women fought dwarfs and men crossed sabres, after which Figg, following displays with sword, dagger, buckler and quarter staff, would box. The grotesque shows flourished as his sporting retreat attracted the full spectrum of London life. Figg's gruesome exhibitions are part of boxing's bloody and savage heritage.

In the 1720s Figg fought Ned Sutton from Kent. It was a challenge, a duel in three stages. First there was the backsword, followed by a break for port; second was the pugilism section and finally, after another break for port, the cudgels were used. Figg broke Sutton's knee to win. Contemporary accounts create a vivid image of the fighting. Figg was bleeding heavily before winning and several people fainted!

▲ ACTION WAS RARE!

Top: A good deal of moving and posing was common in 18th-century fights. Many of the contests lasted for hours, but the action was usually limited to quick flurries, throws and pulls.

▲ DEDICATED TO THE FANCY

Showrooms for gentlemen to punch each other opened up all over London in the early part of the 19th century. Poets and dandies were instructed in the manly art of self-defence by retired prizefighters.

MILESTONES OF BOXING
· · · · · · · · · · · · · · · ·
JACK BROUGHTON'S RULES
1743

Boxing's first rules were read to a gathering of pugilists by Jack Broughton in August 1743. The seven rules were written by Broughton and Captain John Godfrey.

The rules were not designed to help the sport of boxing, but to promote interest from the gambling fraternity, whose support was crucial to the sport's development.

Following the implementation of the rules, fighters were permitted just 30 seconds to recover and get back to the line for the next round. Broughton was given the right to enter the ring to restore "decorum" in rule three, while rule six dealt with the selection of two officials "to decide all disputes." Boxing bouts needed clean finishes, the gamblers needed a clear winner and the rules provided this. Only rule seven dealt with the fighting itself, by excluding grabbing a man below the waist and hitting an adversary "when he is down." There was no mention, even in those days, of more creative infringements such as biting an opponent's ear!

▶ **FATHERS OF THE FIST**

Jack Broughton (left) and James Figg (right) never fought. Instead both men ran their theatres of the physically grotesque from the safety of the stage.

Boxing was one of the more civilized attractions at the Boarded House

Jack Broughton was known as the father of modern pugilism. His rules, which were essentially gambling concessions, were written by himself and Captain Godfrey and published in August 1743. Godfrey also wrote boxing's first book.

Broughton had first fought in the many sporting booths in central London, but took over the Boarded House in 1743. Two years earlier he had been involved in a fight at the booths with George Stevenson, which ended with modern boxing's first death, when Stevenson died some weeks later in Broughton's arms.

Many have sought to link the birth of the rules with a desire to safeguard the sport after Stevenson's death, but in truth Broughton was an entrepreneur and without rules and guidelines the sport would have continued to be dogged by unsatisfactory

conclusions to fights and was therefore in danger of losing its gamblers. The rules helped persuade gentlemen gamblers, wealthy merchants and royal patrons to continue their support of pugilism.

Broughton enticed his fans with theatrical sideshows at the Boarded House and in 1748 he opened a boxing academy in the Haymarket, London, where gloves, or "mufflers", as they were known, were first used. Broughton started a tradition for performers in the "manly art" to earn money away from the ring as trainers to the rich and famous. His newspaper advertisements claimed: "Persons of quality and distinction will be given the utmost tenderness, for which reasons mufflers are provided, that will effectually secure them from the inconveniency of black eyes, broken jaws and bloody noses."

▲ MEN OF DISTINCTION

The sparring sessions at Fives Court in London took place in the middle of the Real Tennis court, in this case involving Randall and Turpin in 1805. Boxing was an important part of the sporting revolution at the end of the 18th century and later during the first half of the 19th century.

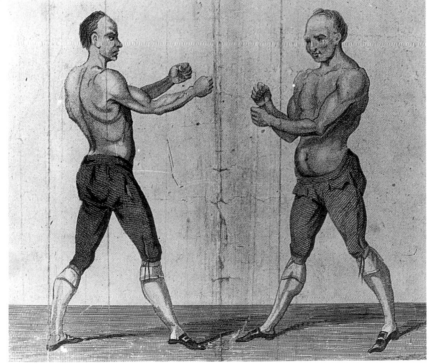

◄ HEROES OF THE FIST

Jack Broughton and Jack Slack fighting on April 10, 1750. The fight only lasted 14 minutes with Broughton defeated when his eyes were closed by Slack's punches. Broughton's patron, the Duke of Cumberland, was most upset – the odds on a Slack win were high.

The Queensberry Rules saved the sport from the Victorian bruisers

▶ **CRIBB V MOLINEAUX**

There was more than a title at stake when Tom Molineaux arrived in Britain from America in 1809. Upon arrival he sought and found another freed slave, Bill Richmond. After the rematch with Cribb, it was alleged that Richmond (pictured standing behind Molineaux) had dissuaded his man from training hard.

From Broughton's retirement, in 1754, until the Queensberry Rules in 1867, prizefighting went through varying stages of popularity, but the steady arrival of black fighters from America and the West Indies created much interest.

One such immigrant was Tom Molineaux. In 1810, Molineaux, a former slave, was cheated out of victory when he met champion Tom Cribb. Cribb was knocked senseless in round 28, prompting his cornerman, Jem Ward, to walk across to Molineaux's corner during the 30 second break and strike up a debate. He was possibly trying to increase the bet. At any rate, the ruse worked and Cribb was given extra time to recover – he went on to win in round 34.

Angelo Dundee did the same thing when he helped tear Cassius Clay's glove after a brutal knockdown against Britain's Henry Cooper in 1963. Clay was also given extra time to recover.

The rematch between Cribb and Molineaux in 1811 was watched by over 20,000 spectators. However, Molineaux was weary from a publicity tour and was easily beaten in 11 rounds.

By the 1860s a new sport was needed. "These fellows are, indeed, amongst the curiosities of civilization", wrote one spectator. In 1860, the great international fight between America's John Heenan and Britain's Tom Sayers ended in confusion when Sayers quit the ring. It was bare-knuckle prize fighting's first grand goodbye. A newspaper of the time called it "a blot upon the social history of the year." That history soon underwent a drastic change with the introduction of the Queensberry Rules.

The black immigrant, Tom Molineaux, is pictured breaking Capt. Robert Barclay's ribs during a sparring session. Capt. Barclay was the most prolific trainer from the period and trained a number of athletes. Tom Cribb hired Barclay to train him for his return fight with Molineaux.

MILESTONES OF BOXING

· · · · · · · · · · · · · · · ·

BOXING'S FIRST BOOK

In 1747 Captain John Godfrey's *A Treatise upon the Useful Science of Defence* was published. Such was its appeal that fakes appeared the very same year.

Godfrey was a friend of Broughton, but had first trained under James Figg, and was also an accomplished swordsman and renowned man about town. He introduced Broughton to the Duke of Cumberland, who was later to become the prizefighter's backer!

The descriptions in the book of a boxer's balance are still valid today. Godfrey was obsessed as a boxer and swordsman with gravity, the proper distance between the legs. "A less degree of Art will tell far more than a considerably greater strength. Strength is certainly what the boxer ought to set out with, but without Art he will succeed but poorly."

DEMPSEY V FIRPO

Boxing's Most Ferocious Round

▶ **THE FINAL KNOCKDOWN**

Dempsey walks away from the stricken Luis Angel Firpo after the ninth and final knockdown. "I knew it was the last time" said Dempsey after the fight, "He had taken too many and would not take any more."

▼ **A SAVAGE NIGHT FOR FIRPO**

Dempsey and Firpo met to dispute Dempsey's world heavyweight championship in 1923. Firpo found there was no way out and, after the notorious first round, proceedings came to a sudden halt in round two.

The press at the time claimed the "last shred of civilization had snapped", during round one of the Jack Dempsey-Luis Angel Firpo heavyweight title fight at the Polo Grounds, New York, in September 1923. It was boxing's second million-dollar fight and arguably the sport's most ferocious round.

"Blood thirsty savages watching a struggle to the death between two fight-crazy maniacs", was how one journalist described the action. By the end of the first minute of round two, Firpo had been dropped nine times, the final time for the full count, while Dempsey had been knocked through the ropes and saved by the outstretched hands of dumbstruck sportswriters.

"The bell rang right away and that saved me", recalled Dempsey nearly 50 years later. When he was thrown back in the ring he was too dazed to move from the ropes and Firpo lost his chance when the bell was somehow heard above the howls of the 82,000 crowd.

Tex Rickard needed the Dempsey-Firpo fight to be a success. Two months earlier Dempsey and his manager, Doc Kearns, had fled from the town of Shelby, Montana in the hour after Dempsey outpointed Tommy Gibbons, when the town – which had put up the finance – was bankrupted by the flop. Before leaving, Kearns had cleared the final $56,000 from the gate receipts. The Firpo fight restored Rickard's reputation as sport's top promoter, with Dempsey, sport's richest prize, at his side.

Rickard matched Firpo with Jess Willard in Jersey City, just a few days after the Dempsey-Gibbons fiasco in Montana. Firpo won in eight rounds and the dream fight with Dempsey picked up momentum. Earlier attempts to foist Firpo, whom Rickard claimed he discovered in Argentina, on the boxing writers had failed. Beating Willard somehow convinced the cynics.

When it came to fighting Dempsey, however, Firpo was simply too tough for his own limited skills and went down on one knee at the start of the first round. He was then caught with a left hook and went down again. From that moment, until the final 30 seconds of the fight, Firpo was down six more times. Some were clean knockdowns and some the result of Dempsey's fury and his knack of standing directly above a stricken boxer.

After seven knockdowns Firpo landed a desperate lunge to Dempsey's chest and then a right. The world champion tipped from the ring, his feet flipping up as his body sank onto the ringside press tables. He was hurt but he scrambled back, with the help of the writers. Firpo's last effort to end the fight in the few seconds remaining of the first round failed. In the second Firpo was over twice more, the final time from a right, for the full count. The fight was over.

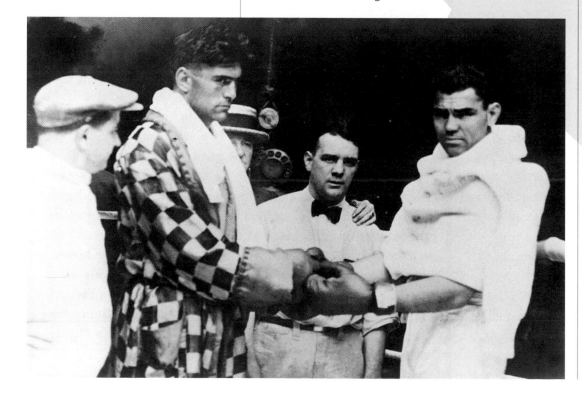

In New York, Jack "Kid" Berg was seen as a new lord from an old land

▲ **THE BOY FROM THE EAST**
Jack "Kid" Berg was born in London's East End. He was called the Whitechapel Whirlwind, and had an immediate impact in New York, winning 14 of his 15 fights between May 1929 and January 1930. Berg's showmanship raised his profile to cult status.

When Benny Leonard retired from the lightweight division in 1925, Tony Canzoneri was just starting. Between Leonard and Henry Armstrong a succession of brilliant lightweights won and lost titles and fights.

Tony Canzoneri was one of the best, becoming only the sixth fighter to win world titles at three weights – feather, lightweight and junior-welterweight – during a time when good fighters fought the best opposition at regular intervals, and often at short

▲ **BERG SHOWS NO FEAR**
In one fight, against Billy Pertrolle in 1930, Berg returned to his corner after round one having been subjected to a thunderous body shot. Asked by his concerned trainer, Ray Arcel, how he felt, the fearless Berg replied, "Lovely thank you. And you?"

MILESTONES OF BOXING

• • • • • • • • • • • • • • • •

THE FIRST MILLION-DOLLAR PURSE

Gene Tunney was once described as "a book-reading dude" by a contemporary journalist. He is seldom described as a great fighter yet when he retired in 1929 he had lost just once in 87 fights. He was clearly a calculated boxer.

In 1926, when he beat Dempsey, he was paid $200,000. His payment for the rematch was a much more complicated affair. Tunney was initially given $999,445 for the fight. He then wrote Rickard a cheque for $9,555 and was in return paid with a cheque for one million dollars. The rematch – a controversial match which Tunney won – was watched by 104,943 eager spectators and took $2,658,660 in gate receipts.

Tunney left the ring for good after beating Tom Heeney in 1928. He never wandered back, never had the urge to fight again that so many former champions had had before and after him. Tunney was content with his money and his glory.

notice. It was an active scene. Not necessarily a fair time, but a time of terrific matches. Few fighters won world titles with unbeaten records before the 1960s.

In early 1930 Canzoneri lost a decision to Britain's Jack "Kid" Berg. The same year Berg, who at the time was only 21, put an end to Kid Chocolate's unbeaten run of 160 fights. Berg was a cult fighter, a brilliant showman whose career was effectively over by the time he was 23.

In 1928 Berg arrived in America. By 1930 he was the champion of the junior-welterweight division, which was not at that time universally recognized. Nevertheless, Berg and his non-stop style had a large following. In New York's Madison Square Garden, the fighter from London's East End proved a huge attraction with nearly 20,000 paying to see his first performance in 1929.

Berg entered the ring wearing a sacred Jewish shawl, a *tallith*, and strips of leather, *tvillan*, strapped to his arms (*tvillan* are a reminder of god's presence). It took Berg several minutes to remove the religious items and after he had kissed each *tvillan*, his trainer, Ray Arcel, would place them in an embroidered, velvet bag. The crowd loved it.

◄ **SWEET SMELL OF SUCCESS**

Tony Canzoneri was a remarkable fighter. During his career he held three world titles, fought 22 championship fights at four different weights and lost only 24 times in 141 fights between 1925 and 1929. He fought the full list of greats from a period of excellence: Johnny Dundee, Lou Ambers, Sammy Mandell, Billy Petrolle, Kid Chocolate, Jack "Kid" Berg, Barney Ross and Jimmy McLarnin.

SHORT-TERM HEAVYWEIGHT CHAMPIONS
Boxing's Time-dishonoured Tradition

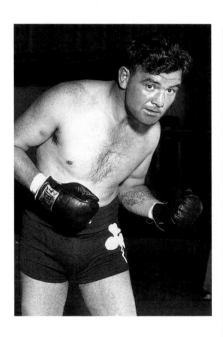

▲ **BRADDOCK'S FAIRYTALE**

James J. Braddock was an unlikely heavyweight champion. His career appeared to be over in the early 1930s, but wins in late 1934 and early 1935 resurrected his fading hopes. In June 1935 his dream came true when he beat Max Baer to win the championship.

From the moment Gene Tunney's left fist started to tame Jack Dempsey, until a night 10 years later when James J.Braddock collapsed against Joe Louis, the heavyweight scene was awash with controversial figures and events. The first fighter to emerge after Tunney was Jack Sharkey who, having beaten top black fighters Harry Wills and George Godfrey in 1926, was knocked out by Dempsey in 1927 as he turned to the referee. Until that moment Sharkey was winning the fight. "What the hell was he doing looking away", asked Dempsey. It was the question on everyone's lips.

In 1930 Sharkey lost a vacant heavyweight title fight when he landed a low blow, a short left hook, and Max Schmeling, a German with a Jewish-American manager, fell in agony to the floor. It was the first time the heavyweight title was won on a foul. It was an accident, but many fights at the time were decided on intentional fouls.

In boxing's time-dishonoured tradition, the title split after Sharkey's fist plunged deep into Schmeling's groin. Schmeling was the linear champion, but in 1931 Primo Carnera was matched with Sharkey for a version of the championship. The Italian lost – a surprise considering the men who controlled his career.

In 1932 Sharkey beat Schmeling in a rematch. There was an outcry from Schmeling's manager, Joe Jacobs, and one of boxing's most often quoted expressions entered the sporting lexicon. As Schmeling ducked his head in defeat Jacobs screamed in disgust: "We wuz robbed – we shoulda stood in bed."

The Sharkey-Carnera rematch was made for June 1933. It was a strange fight from the start and in round six it ended with Sharkey on the canvas. It was another setback. Nobody had faith in Carnera's abilities, but he was now the champion. Mickey Walker, who fought at a lighter weight altogether, beat better heavyweights, but in the 1930s anything went.

Light-heavyweight champion Tommy Loughran is a perfect example of the confusing state of the sport at this time. Loughran fought a no decision bout with Tunney in 1922 and beat Georges Carpentier, Harry Greb, Mickey Walker, Johnny Risko, Ernie Schaaf, King Levinsky, Young Stribling and future heavyweight champions, James J. Braddock and Max Baer. He fought Greb six times (with one win, two losses, one draw and two no decision affairs) and claimed that Tunney refused him a rematch on five occasions.

Loughran was knocked out by Sharkey in 1929 but beat him in a rematch after the Boston Gob, as Sharkey was known, lost his title to Carnera. In 1934 Loughran lost on points to the Italian, whose ring sobriquet, the Ambling Alp, was often referred to as an exaggeration of his speed!

After Carnera came Max Baer, who beat Carnera in the same way Dempsey beat Willard. In 1935 Baer lost to Braddock. The carnival had turned bizarre. Braddock, understandably dubbed the Cinderella Man, had lost 11 of his previous 20 fights before he toyed with Baer. He could fight though; he was an old-fashioned grafter. Braddock should have fought Schmeling but 1937 was a difficult time and the pair never met. Braddock's manager Joe Gould claimed he spoke personally to Joseph Goebbels about the proposed fight. Joe Louis, however, had other plans for Schmeling, in the shape of a revenge bid for his painful first defeat in 1936 when Schmeling knocked him out.

It was only a matter of time before Louis was matched with Braddock. After a gap of 24 months the fight was made and Louis won in 8 rounds in June 1937. Tunney, Schmeling, Sharkey, Carnera, Baer and Braddock had managed just five successful defences between them in 11 years.

▲ **ON DANGEROUS GROUND**
Max Schmeling shaking hands with New York governor Franklin D. Roosevelt before his rematch with Jack Sharkey in 1932.

▲ **BAER AND TUNNEY**
Max Baer (top) had his day in the sun as champion while ignoring most of pugilism's sacred rules. His clowning antics may have endeared him to the fans, but it ultimately ruined his career. By contrast, Gene Tunney (above) was a consummate artist. "I've seen Dempsey fight and I was impressed with his lack of knowledge", he said before outpointing him in 1926.

When Louis and Armstrong entered the ring quality fighters suffered

▲ **LOUIS IS NOT AMUSED**

Joe Louis was not one to smile easily. He was certainly not amused by the grinning Primo Carnera at the scales before their 1935 fight. Carnera was ruined in six rounds. The ruthless Louis also disposed of Max Baer in four rounds and Jack Sharkey in three, but in 1936 he was unexpectedly beaten by Max Schmeling.

In 1931 Tony Canzoneri knocked out "Kid" Berg and later in the year outpointed him, although Berg was still considered world super-lightweight champion by *The Ring* until 1932. Berg started to box at the age of 14 at Premierland, not far from where he was born in London's Whitechapel.

He was in decline after the last Canzoneri fight and although he continued to win, he was never the same. "Berg could tear the hearts out of the toughest pugs", claimed Arcel. Sadly, his timing faded and Berg, like so many others, lost his edge at an early age.

It was a time of transition. There were still relics from the past but increasingly fighters were starting to look more and more modern. Television was just a few years away and stars were needed to fulfil a new role on the small screen. It was possibly the last period of innocence for boxing. At the end of the decade, revenue from television and the manipulative

powers of businessmen and influential organizations started to form the bloody business of boxing that we have today.

By 1937 two new fighters, Henry Armstrong and Joe Louis, had become established and during the next few years they would dominate the sport. At the same time, a young kid called Walker Smith was dazzling the experts in New York's gyms. In the competitive ring, Smith used the name Ray Robinson, Sugar Ray. In the late 1930s boxing's future was secure in the fists of this trio of great fighters. In the 1940s, Rocky Graziano, Tony Zale, Jake La Motta and Marcel Cerdan – whose battles are still used to measure levels of heart, sacrifice and brutality in the boxing ring – would take over their mantle. The middleweights would have their glorious time but in 1937, The Brown Bomber, Joe Louis, was the only fighter who really mattered.

◄ CANZONERI BOWS OUT

Tony Canzoneri decided to quit the ring when he was knocked out in 1939. It was his first stoppage in an incredible career. "There is no point in another fight", he said.

▼ HANK THE HOBO WARRIOR

This publicity shot of Henry Armstrong was taken at Joe Louis's training camp in Pompton Lakes, New Jersey, just before he won the second of his three world titles in 1938. Armstrong's career was a genuine rags to riches story.

THE OTHER SIDE OF BOXING
PRIMO CARNERA

Carnera was never meant to be a fighter. He was discovered in Italy by French sports entrepreneur, Leon See, and guided like a hopeless child from obscurity to the championship by men with the right connections. He beat opponents who were told to lose during a shameful time in boxing's history. Carnera's great love was food and he often met the press in restaurants, hence the many pictures of him eating.

Carnera is famous as the mob's fighter and sadly his legacy has done more to shape the perception of boxing than that of most fighters. Many people are familiar with the story of Primo Carnera, but few know about James J. Braddock, whose journey from the docks and poverty to the world heavyweight title during the same period was a much happier affair.

Following a succession of fixed fights, Carnera won the heavyweight title by beating Jack Sharkey in unconvincing fashion in 1933. Following two successful defences, he was soundly beaten by Max Baer the next year. The end of Carnera was easy to predict and his free fall, once it was obvious the game was up, remains one of boxing's most disgraceful incidents. He eventually turned to wrestling, all 6ft 7in and 260 pounds of fragile Italian granite.

★ ★

LOUIS
and Hank

1937-1945

★ ★

Armstrong's triple success will never be repeated

▶ ARMSTRONG V GARCIA

Ceferino Garcia (left) and Henry Armstrong met for the first time in 1938. Armstrong retained his welterweight title on that occasion, but in 1940 they drew in a fight for the middleweight title. "It was never easy with Henry" said Garcia, "he was punching and moving all the time."

In the late 1930s the lightweight division had a number of quality champions – among them Tony Canzoneri, Lou Ambers and Henry Armstrong – and surprisingly few weak links. "Them were the good old days", claimed Lou Ambers years later.

Ambers began as a bootleg fighter for $5. In 1938, he lost his lightweight championship to Henry Armstrong but won it back the following year. Both fights were hard and the second dirty – Armstrong's illegal punches costing him five rounds and the title. A mooted third fight never happened. When Ambers was stopped by Lew Jenkins in 1940 for the New York version of the championship, he was only 26. Nearly 100 fights had taken their toll and he was old in ring years before his time. "When a fellow gets old in this game, you're going to weaken", he acknowledged.

Beau Jack – another promising lightweight of the period – was 21 when he won the New York version of the title. Jack was the main attraction at Madison Square Garden 21 times, beating Tippy Larkin for the title and then winning just one of three title fights with Bob Montgomery between 1943 and 1944. In 1944 Jack beat Montgomery, who at the time was still champion, in a non-title fight as part of a war bonds drive. Jack, who started and ended his working life shining shoes, first boxed in Battle Royals, a form of boxing that owed more to the entertainment values of the ancient Romans than war-time boxing. In a Battle Royal, four or five black fighters would be blindfolded and would slug away until just two were left. Then they would box. Armstrong had refused to take part in Battle Royals, but Jack had little alternative.

▲ "MAIN EVENT" JACK

Armstrong was in the twilight days of his fighting life when he met Beau Jack (right) at Madison Square Garden in April 1943. Jack held the New York version of the world lightweight title at the time and had just beaten Fritzie Zivic. During his career, Jack fought in 21 main events at Madison Square Garden in front of a total of 335,000 fight fans.

◄ THE HERKIMER HURRICANE

Lou Ambers found the bright lights after years in boxing's wilderness – winning and losing the world lightweight title on two occasions between 1936 and 1940. He had started fighting in boxing booths, where he fought more than 150 times. His record in the ring was 86 wins, eight losses and six draws.

57

DAYS OF *Sugar*

1945-1952

Sugar Ray Robinson was one of the greats and was involved in many fights that will forever be remembered as among boxing's finest. He held history in his fists for nearly 20 years and shaped generations, to whom he was a role model, hero and genius in the ring.

ROBINSON: THE NEW BABE

▲ A BAD END

Freddie Mills could take a beating. He was on the wrong end of several savage attacks before winning the world light-heavyweight title in 1948, when he outpointed American veteran Gus Lesnevich. In 1965 Mills was found shot dead in an alley behind his club in London's Soho.

◀ ROBINSON SPARKLES

Previous page: Sugar Ray pictured in training at Blooms Gymnasium in London's West End.

Sugar Ray Robinson was the sweetest thing to enter a boxing ring. His long career and fights against former, present and past world champions amount to possibly the finest record ever accomplished by a fighter. He won his first world title fight in 1946 and lost his last in 1961. Boxing changed to such an extent during Robinson's career that when he finally retired in 1965 he was a living icon to a sport that many believed would never be as good again.

His first few years as champion – when he won the welterweight, the middleweight and failed in the most dramatic way to win Joey Maxim's light-heavyweight championship in 1952 – were his best.

Robinson was not alone, however, he fought alongside a number of other legends. Just as Robinson was in the ascendant, Joe Louis was winding down. At the end of World War II, Louis had aged, his face losing its youthful appearance after the four-year break. In 1946, Louis met and soundly beat Billy Conn in a rematch, but his timing was not what it had been.

One fight each in 1947 and 1948, both against Jersey Joe Walcott, kept Louis in the public eye but he was starting to look and fight like an old man. In 1949 Louis quit but his absence was temporary and in 1950 he lost for only the second time when Ezzard Charles, the new heavyweight champion, outpointed him over 15 gruelling rounds.

At the same time Rocky Marciano was just starting to fight men with reputations. A dubious win over Roland La Starza seemed to suggest, however, that Marciano was not quite ready to move from the safety of easy workouts to the dangers of exposure in harder fights. In 1951 an ideal compromise was found and

Joe Louis, who had won eight in a row since his Charles defeat, was given to Marciano. It was a harder fight than is generally recognized but it ended in round eight. Louis was trapped on the ropes and helpless. It was his last fight. Marciano won the title the next year.

It is Robinson, sometimes known as the Black Angel, who has inspired fighters since the moment he first won a title. He had the style in and away from the ring to alter the way people thought about fighters. However, he was as ruthless as any boxer before or after him. In 1947 Robinson defended his welterweight title for the first time when he met Jimmy Doyle. A left hook to the head dropped Doyle in round eight. He later died in hospital from injuries sustained during the fight. When Robinson was asked by the coroner: "Couldn't you see that Doyle had been hurt and was groggy?", he replied "Mister, that's what my business is – to hurt people." There was criticism for the honest reply and Robinson set up a $10,000 trust fund for Doyle's mother. His critics were numerous and as Muhammad Ali would discover 15 years later, any seemingly callous comment could be taken out of context and used as proof of insensitivity or arrogance.

While Robinson and Louis were at different stages in their careers, the business of boxing was under the control of the gangsters. Fixed fights were nothing new to boxing, but in the late 1940s and throughout the 1950s, the entire business operated under a dark cloud of corrupt officials.

In January 1947 Rocky Graziano, less than four months after losing a world middleweight title fight to Tony Zale, was questioned at the DA's office in New York about an attempt to bribe him to lose a fight. Graziano denied the bribe offer was serious. "It was just some punk talking to me on the phone. It never meant nothing", Graziano claimed. The DA disagreed, informed the New York State Athletic Commission and in February 1947 Graziano's licence to fight in his native city was revoked.

In April Graziano's attempt to regain his status in New York failed but in July of the same year, fighting under an Illinois licence, he knocked Tony Zale out to win the world title. It was a genuine win but Graziano's refusal to take a dive, or "tank a fight", as they called it, only served to heighten the

involvement of the mobsters.

After Graziano beat Zale there was a celebration party in his Chicago hotel room. One of the guests was the notorious gangster Paul John Carbo, alias Frankie Carbo, alias Paul Carbo, alias Frank Carbo, alias Frank Russo, alias John Paul Carbo!

It was Carbo, a man convicted of manslaughter, who came to be recognized, alongside Frank "Blinky" Palermo, as one of the criminal leaders in the boxing business. Some despaired of their influence. Others saw them as pioneers.

In reality, they were just doing business according to one of boxing's oldest maxims: you get what you negotiate, not what you deserve. Both Carbo and Palermo knew a thing or two about negotiating.

▲ **ARMSTRONG V ROBINSON**

"Fight man. I ain't never been booed in the Garden", said Henry Armstrong (right) to Sugar Ray Robinson when they met at Madison Square Garden on August 27, 1943. Robinson won on points after 10 rounds of calculated boxing, beating his hero while never once risking defeat.

Money problems force Louis's return

▲ SO CLOSE TO THE END

Joe Louis almost lost his fight with Jersey Joe Walcott in 1947. He felt like an old man, but in their rematch in June 1948, Louis (right) stopped Walcott in round 11. It was to be Louis's 25th and last defence of the world heavyweight championship. He retired the following year, but soon returned.

Too many fighters neglect the signs of disintegration and continue fighting. Joe Louis, sadly, was one of them.

When Louis defended his title against Jersey Joe Walcott in 1947 he won a close and disputed decision. Walcott had been a sparring partner in the Louis camp in 1938 but, despite the outcome of the fight, it was obvious time had been kinder to the understudy.

Louis was over twice, in rounds one and four, and tried to leave the ring before the decision was announced. "I made it tough. I saw openings I didn't use. I beat him, but next time I will knock him out", promised Louis. The rematch was in 1948 and Louis fulfilled his promise, knocking Walcott out in round 11. It was the 25th and last title defence of Louis's 11 years as champion.

When Louis retired the following year, he was undefeated champion. Unfortunately tax problems forced him to make a comeback when he should have been enjoying his retirement. In 1950 he was back. He challenged Ezzard Charles, who held a version of the championship, for the vacant world title. Louis was paid $9,000 less for this fight than he had received for winning the title from James J. Braddock in 1937. His tax problems remained.

Charles won easily and hurt Louis on several occasions. When it was over, Charles said: "I never wanted to hurt the old fellow who did so much for the Negro in boxing." But he still left Louis stumbling. However, it was not the end. That awful night would come 13 months later against Rocky Marciano.

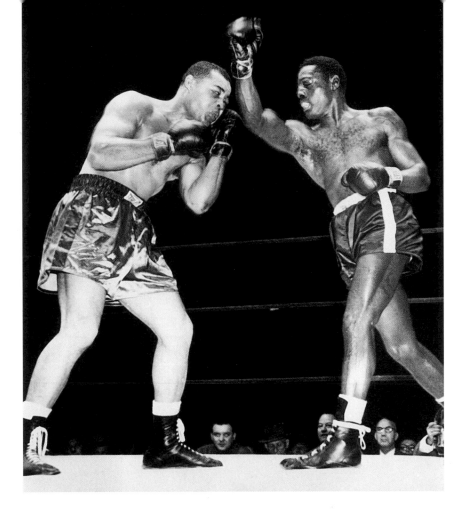

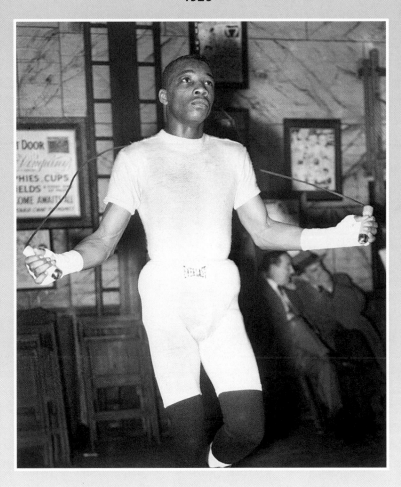

GIANTS OF THE RING

· · · · · · · · · · · · · · · ·

SANDY SADDLER

1926–

It is hard to imagine just what goes through Sandy Saddler's head each time he is introduced as a "former featherweight champion of the world." The comment hardly does him justice. He also held the junior-lightweight title but he was much more than a champion. He was quite simply brilliant.

His four fights with Willie Pep are proof. When he had to adjust against Pep he was clever. His timing was perfect and his arms were long enough to surprise many opponents from the edge of the ring. His last featherweight defence in 1956 – eight years after first winning the title – against Gabriel "Flash" Elorde, from the Philippines, is an indication of just how great he was. Saddler stopped Elorde in round 13. It was revenge for a non-title fight points defeat the year before.

▲ **A FADED FORMER CHAMP**

Louis came out of retirement to be beaten up by Ezzard Charles in a world title fight in September 1950 (top). Charles won the contest easily, but Louis refused to fade away and came back to face Lee Savold the following year.

▲ **LOUIS DESTROYS SAVOLD**

A battered Lee Savold (above left) tumbles down the ropes after Louis's final onslaught of punches in June 1951. Savold had won a version of the world title after Louis retired in 1949, but Charles was considered the true champion.

CHARLEY BURLEY

Burley's Sorrow, Boxing's Shame

Few names cause as much wonder and confusion in the history of boxing as Charley Burley. He was without doubt one of the sport's greats, possibly the best fighter never to win a world title. In 1992 partial justice was served when Burley was made a member of Boxing's Hall of Fame, but a position next to the champions from the 1930s, 1940s and 1950s is scant reward for a fighter who was never given a chance because he was black, honest and simply too good for his peers.

Burley's class is obvious from his record and there are many, including veteran trainers Ray Arcel and Eddie Futch, who make bold claims on Burley's behalf. They certainly agree he was the best fighter never to win a title and they should know, as their association with boxing started in the 1920s.

Sugar Ray Robinson was the most famous fighter to avoid Burley. According to Burley, he was offered a fight with Robinson if he took a dive in the first round. Futch has also claimed that Robinson would not fight Burley. Their careers overlap and they could have fought in 1943 or 1944 but by the time Robinson was champion at welterweight, Burley was possibly too big, and when Robinson was middleweight champion it was too late for him.

In 1938 Burley won and lost in fights with Fritzie Zivic and beat him again in 1939. The same year, Zivic won the world welterweight title from Henry Armstrong. To add insult to the injustice Zivic, while champion, actually bought Burley's contract which meant he managed the man he should have been fighting! Sense got the better of Zivic's conscience,

however, and Burley was soon back to fighting bigger men. In 1938 he beat Billy Soose and in 1940 Soose beat world middleweight champion Tony Zale in a non-title fight. He claimed the title the following year.

Burley fought Holman Williams – another black fighter who never quite got his break – a total of seven times. They each won three with one no-contest. Burley also lost twice to Ezzard Charles on points in 1942. In 1944, however, Burley beat Archie Moore. Veteran trainer Eddie Futch remembers the night: "Burley left work, went home, got his gear, hopped on a bus, came up the 125 miles to Hollywood, went into the ring, and gave Archie a good 10-round licking." Moore has never disputed the beating, and once described Burley's style as "slick as lard and twice as greasy." "I wasn't that big but I could beat the heavyweights. I knew when their punches was coming, let it miss, slip a little and then start punching", Burley later added.

Charley Burley could have and should have won a world title. It was a time of ferocious competition and even more savage discrimination, but despite this he held a world ranking from 1939 until 1946, first in the welterweight top five and then in the middleweight top three. In 1947 Burley, who was 30, had to go to work as a garbage collector because he had trouble finding opponents. As Burley himself commented, "It was never easy for me. I could see what was happening but what could I do if people never wanted to fight me. I could get close to a title, have people tell me it was gonna happen, but it just never fell the right way for me in the end."

Before Burley died in 1992 he was asked what would have happened if Robinson had agreed to fight him. "He woulda been in trouble. I guess I woulda been, too. Ray ducked me. I wanted him. But it wasn't for me."

◄ **THE TALENTED OUTCAST**
Charley Burley was highly rated, and avoided for that very reason. In 1942, future world heavyweight champion, Ezzard Charles outpointed him twice but never stopped him. Archie Moore said he was the hardest man he had ever fought. He gained respect despite being sidelined and died in 1992, shortly after being inducted into the Boxing Hall of Fame in Canastota, New York.

The YEARS *of Rock*

1952-1964

After Joe Louis, Ezzard Charles and Jersey Joe Walcott came Rocky Marciano. The heavyweight title was often in a lull in the few years between the demise of Louis and the emergence of Marciano and his relentless pursuit of blood. Archie Moore proved to be the sentinel at the edge of changing history.

ROCKY TIMES

▲ THE OLD WARRIOR MOORE

Some people say that Archie Moore had two birthdays each year – one his real age, the other his fighting age (which was allegedly three years younger). He was certainly old in boxing years when he fought for the heavyweight championship.

◄ THE ROCK AND MOORE

Previous page: Marciano misses with a wild uppercut during the third round of his fight with Moore.

Rocky Marciano once said: "In a fight you just go in there and go crazy if necessary." The strategy obviously worked given that he never let himself down in any of his 49 fights and was able to retire as undefeated world heavyweight champion in 1956.

After his famous victory over Louis, Marciano's next fight was with Jersey Joe Walcott for the title. Walcott had become the oldest man to win the championship when, at the fifth attempt, he beat Ezzard Charles in 1951. The fight with Marciano should have been in New York but it was switched to Philadelphia because Felix Bocchicchio, Walcott's manager, was suspended in New York for having a criminal record. "If I lose to Marciano take my name out of the record books", said Walcott, "He is not even good enough to be in Joe Louis's 'Bum of the Month Club.'" As usual, Marciano said little and left the talking to his manager, Al Weill, and trainer, Charlie Goldman.

Marciano and Walcott met in September 1952. In the first round Marciano was down from a left hook, but he was up on the count of two, ready to go crazy. Walcott, however, was skilled in survival and made Marciano look foolish again and again before age and Marciano's ability to absorb punishment started to alter the fight. In round nine Walcott was dropped, in round 10 he looked like the old man he was and in round 13 a right, an infamous Marciano "Suzy Q", landed and Walcott was down and out.

One ringside journalist said the sickening final punch left Walcott "looking down his own spine with eyes that could not see." The punch is one of the most famous in boxing's history. Walcott never stood a chance. At the time of the knockout he was leading on all three scorecards. A rematch was inevitable and when they met eight months later it was over in one round. There was nothing Walcott could do, he was caught cold. However, Sugar Ray Robinson was critical, saying Walcott "Not only let his people down, he sat on them." He never fought again.

Walcott had been an odd champion. When he won the title in 1951, it was his 21st year as a pro. "Boxing was a mystery to me. When I look back and see what I had to go through to get to the top I find it hard to believe", Walcott reflected after he retired. In his last fight with Marciano, when he was 39, he looked older than any heavyweight had ever done in a championship fight.

For Archie Moore 1952 was the year he had been waiting for. "I should have been champion of the world as a middleweight round about 1940 when I was 23", said Moore, who claimed to be three years younger than his mother said he was. Instead, he had a long wait until he finally got Joey Maxim in the ring. Moore won over 15 rounds. The pair would repeat the fight and the decision in both 1953 and 1954.

Moore was extraordinary in many ways. After beating Maxim he set his sights on Marciano, taking out adverts in newspapers and pursuing the champion in much the same way as Jack Johnson had done with Tommy Burns. Moore wore capes, excessive outfits and twirled canes. Marciano disliked Moore's style but the pair were kept in separate arenas until 1955. Even in defeat Moore was a showman. If he was bruised, cut or sore he would still attempt to entertain. After losing to Marciano he stood on a table at the post-fight press conference: "Gentlemen", he said addressing the press, "I hope you enjoyed that as much as I did."

In the same year, Sugar Ray Robinson made a comeback, but he had been fighting for too many years. He lost his second fight and was on the canvas in another. However, his form improved and he won and lost the middleweight title three times between 1955 and 1960. Many of the fights have a special place in the sentimental archives of all who sought the sacred in Robinson: the two with Carmen Basilio, in particular, are unforgettable.

When the titles were gone, the last fights – often against good young boxers – went on too long. Had Robinson stopped boxing some years earlier he would have undoubtedly become the icon he is today long before he actually lost his last fight in November 1965. He started boxing when Joe Louis had been heavyweight champion for three years and quit when Muhammad Ali was in his second year as champion.

Robinson's last fight, against contender Joey Archer, ended in a points defeat, but Archer was world-class and 12 months earlier had outpointed Dick Tiger. When Archer beat Robinson there was a new middleweight champion – it was Tiger. Robinson was still able to mix with the best in his division when he was 45 years old.

The influence of the gangsters and wiseguys, whose colourful careers had covered roughly the same period as Robinson's fighting years, was also in decline during this time and many were forced to retire early. A Senate Committee Hearing in 1957 found Jim Norris, his associates and the IBC guilty of monopolistic practices. The game was up. In 1959 the Supreme Court ordered the "divestment, dissolution and divorcement" of Jim Norris's International Boxing

Club from the sport of professional boxing. Norris's reaction was to offer J. Edgar Hoover a $100,000 salary to salvage the IBC.

For Frankie Carbo and Blinky Palermo, the plot thickened. The two sporting "gentlemen" were eventually sentenced to 25 and 15 years respectively for trying to extort money from a promoter. Carbo had earlier been sentenced to two years in New York for undercover matchmaking. Their departure only justified the years of complaints by Cus D'Amato, a manager who was frozen out as a result of his insistence on independence.

In 1956 D'Amato found himself in charge of the heavyweight division when his fighter Floyd Patterson won the vacant title by stopping Moore. However, D'Amato was only part saviour and he took the heavyweight championship on a tricky journey in the ensuing years.

▼ **MARCIANO'S "SUZY Q"**
Rocky Marciano lands a trademark "Suzy Q" – big right cross – to flatten Jersey Joe Walcott in round 13 and win the world heavyweight title. At the time of the knockdown Marciano was losing on points.

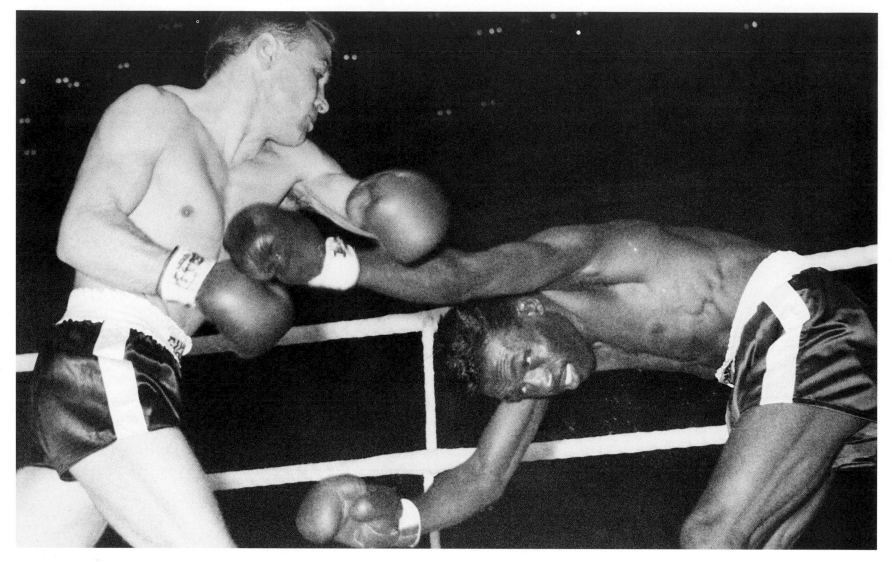

"Just one right hand punch used to break jaws" – Joe Brown

▲ "OLD BONES" BROWN

Joe Brown (right) was 30 when he won the lightweight title, 36 when he lost it and 44 when he finally retired in 1970. In 1959 Brown beat Charnley in Houston, Texas, because of a deep cut, and he repeated the victory in their rematch (above).

Joe Brown, like Archie Moore, fought in four different decades. He was known as "Old Bones", which is surely a perfect description of a man who looked old when he was young and yet somehow managed to defy time when he was old.

Brown was a well-connected man. His manager during his world title years was Lou Viscusi, a friend of Carbo. Brown turned professional in 1943 and fought top-ranked boxers from the start, winning the lightweight title in 1956. His wins over Wallace Smith, Orlando Zulueta, Britain's Dave Charnley, Kenny Lane and Ralph Dupas during his six year reign as champion

make him one of the lightweight greats.

When he lost the title in 1962, he passed the championship to another great fighter, Carlos Ortiz, from Puerto Rico. In their televised fight Ortiz was technically brilliant. He knew that trading punches with Brown, who had a knack of finding the type of punch that could put a swift end to fights, would be foolish. Ortiz had won and lost the junior-welterweight title before meeting Brown and although he was young he was a quality fighter and won after 15 rounds. Brown never got another chance but continued fighting until 1970.

◄ A BLACK DAY FOR BROWN

Brown made hard work of his rematch with Dave Charnley in 1961 and made just one more defence after it. In 1962 he fell victim to Carlos Ortiz in Las Vegas, in a dignified last act.

▲ A TRUE PROFESSIONAL

Brown and Charnley pictured at the weigh-in for their 1961 clash. After losing the title to Ortiz, Brown was back in London in 1963 – this time losing to Charnley in six rounds. By then Brown knew it was over, but he was a true pro – appearing in 41 more fights despite losing 21 of them.

Robinson still tasted as sweet as sugar after his comeback

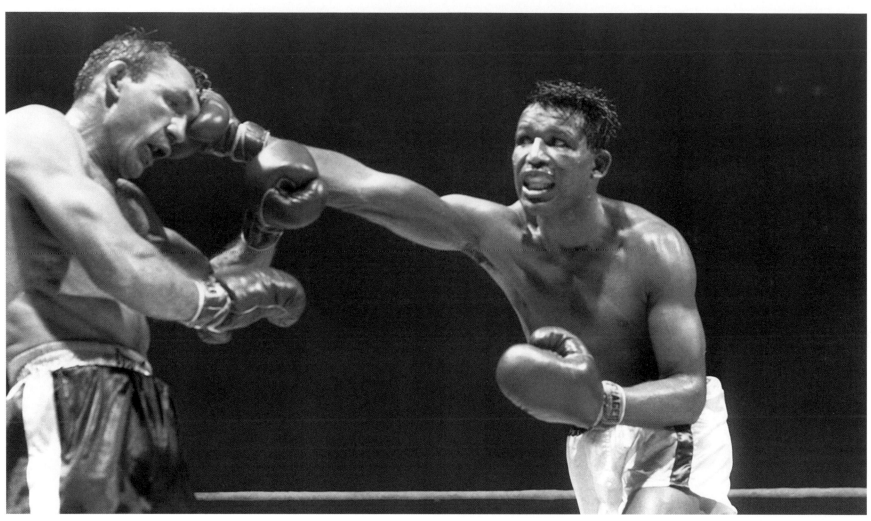

▲ **SUGAR'S SWEET RIGHT**

Robinson's right damages Carmen Basilio in their 1958 rematch. Basilio's left eye was closed from round six and he lost the title he had won just a few months earlier.

The comeback of Sugar Ray Robinson was amazing. At the end of 1955 he knocked out Carl Bobo Olson with a perfect left hook to win the middleweight title again. The form-book was useless when Robinson's punches were finding their mark.

After beating Olson in a return fight in 1956 Robinson had the most remarkable year of his pro career in 1957; it was certainly hard but it confirmed – not that confirmation was necessary – Robinson's position as one of the true greats. In January Robinson lost his title after 15 rounds to Gene Fullmer. There was a rematch clause and this time Robinson, after studying tapes of Fullmer's fights, devised a plan. He saw a gap for a left hook, he told people. The

fight ended in round five with Fullmer on the canvas for the first time in his career: it was the left hook.

Robinson's year was not over yet, however. He was 37 when he defended his title against Carmen Basilio in September 1957. Basilio was the welterweight champion and an uncompromising brawler. The fight was gruesome and when it was over after 15 rounds Basilio was the new champion. One journalist said after the fight: "They may fight again, but they'll never fight any better."

They did meet again and it was as magnificent as the first occasion with Basilio fighting from round six with a swollen eye. At the end of round 15 Robinson was champion once again.

◄ **STYLISH IN TRAINING**

Robinson looking slick in training before his points defeat to Terry Downes, in 1962. He lost three of his six fights that year, and fought in America, Trinidad, France, Austria and England before finally quitting the ring in 1965.

▼ **A SWING OF WILD FURY**

Basilio sways from Robinson's vicious right uppercut early in their second fight. It would be the last world title victory of Robinson's career.

GIANTS OF THE RING
● ● ● ● ● ● ● ● ● ● ● ● ● ● ●
ROCKY MARCIANO
1923–1969

Rocky never officially lost a professional fight. He came close but his sheer guts, combined with the help of the officials on several occasions, saw him through. When it was time to go he left with a perfect record of 49 wins in 49 fights, including 43 by stoppage.

He had the presence of mind to recover when hurt and an instinct that allowed him to get through drastic moments. He also had, in his favoured right hand, a single punch finish. He was not, by any means, a perfect fighting machine but neither was he the "master of no defence", as he was often unjustly dubbed. His reach was 14 inches less than Ali's and even an old Louis had caught him clean. But as a champion he beat the men in front of him and that is all that matters, even if some were not the best available.

Sonny Liston had a face that bore the strain of a lifetime's hardship

▲ A SOLEMN SONNY

Sonny Liston had to wait a long time to prove himself in the ring. But for the politics outside the ropes he would have met Patterson in the 1950s. "I could see what was happening", said Liston "I just had to find the patience to wait." When they did eventually meet in 1962, Liston needed just 126 seconds to win the title.

Sonny Liston was bad news. He had spent time in prison for armed robbery before he was a boxer and served time for assaulting a policeman when he was a boxer. There were many, including former champion Jack Dempsey, who believed he needed to prove himself a worthy citizen before getting his chance at a title. He had already proved himself in the ring.

He should have been given the chance to knock Patterson out in 1960 or 1961, but had to beat Valdes, Machen, Williams and Folley to keep busy. His chance finally came in Chicago in 1962. It was rumoured that Liston was part-owned by Blinky Palermo and Liston was and still is referred to as a "mob fighter." The

connection motivated D'Amato to keep Patterson as far away from him as possible. Patterson had been through reform school and Liston through jail, but there the similarities ended.

On the night the pair met at Comiskey Park, it took Liston just two minutes and six seconds to get what he deserved. "The left had all of me in it", claimed Liston. "The only time I was hurt was when he started getting up on one knee at the count of nine. I thought he was going to make it before 10, which shouldn't happen to anybody I hit." It never did and Patterson was counted out. Liston, so often a guilty man but also a regular fall guy, had justice on his side at last.

▲ THE END OF EASY STREET

Patterson (top) in training for the Liston fight. Liston promised Patterson a mauling. "It will be quick", said the challenger. It was.

▲ OPEN SLAUGHTER

Liston (above right) knows that Patterson is out on his feet as yet another right uppercut is about to rattle the senses of the champion.

GIANTS OF THE RING

• • • • • • • • • • • • • • •

FLOYD PATTERSON

1935–

Patterson will forever be remembered for two unique records he set. In 1956 he beat Archie Moore to become the youngest heavyweight champion at the age of 21, and in 1960 he became the first fighter to regain the heavyweight championship, when he knocked Ingemar Johansson out in their rematch.

Patterson was 17 when he won an Olympic gold medal at middleweight in 1952. His careful rise from amateur star to world champion – there was only a slight problem when he was narrowly outpointed by veteran Joey Maxim – set the standard for the future and angered many of the old purists whose early careers' had been much tougher. It was the end of the old days, when long apprenticeships and hard fights eventually led somewhere. After Patterson came Clay and he needed even less time and fewer fights before he won a world title.

A KID called Clay

1964-1971

His predictions were so often right. When Cassius Clay started to tell the truth the world of boxing was stunned. He was so pretty and so fast that the best were reduced to watching him in disbelief. "He can beat Liston now", said Archie Moore in 1962. He was right.

PURE ALI

▲ THE PERFECT SHADOW

Cassius Marcellus Clay was born in Louisville, Kentucky in 1942. "I'm going to be the perfect champion – like the young Joe Louis. I'm clean living, I haven"t got a prison record. I think you've got to be an idol for young people', said Clay in 1963.

◄ THE "LOUISVILLE LIP"

Previous page: Clay in London for his fight with Cooper in 1963, predicting a fifth-round knockout.

Boxing changed forever in 1964. When Cassius Clay beat Sonny Liston, the Big Ugly Bear, the sport was revitalized, never to be the same again. The morning after his victory, Clay became Cassius X.

After winning a gold at light-heavyweight in the 1960 Rome Olympics, Clay turned professional with the help of a syndicate of businessmen in his home town of Louisville. Known as the Louisville Sponsoring Group, the LSG consisted of 11 white men aged between 25-70; 10 were millionaires and they contributed $2,800 each, while William Faversham, the organizer, contributed just half that amount. Clay received a $10,000 signing bonus.

At first Clay stayed in Louisville where he was trained by Fred Stoner, a black man he had known for years. After his pro debut at the Freedom Hall, Louisville, however, the LSG decided they needed someone with more experience in Clay's corner. Clay wanted Sugar Ray Robinson but he was sent instead to Archie Moore in San Diego.

At Moore's gym, The Bucket of Blood, the young fighter and the old fell out over many things. Clay, for instance, refused to sweep the floor when asked. The pair were from different worlds. Moore had come through hardships that Clay would never have to know and still slept with his watch and wallet under his pillow. Clay left just a few months after arriving.

When the two men eventually fought two years later, Clay had clearly matured and instantly comforted Moore at the end of the bout.

Clay was then sent to Miami to work with Angelo Dundee. The pair had met a few years earlier in Louisville when Clay had pestered Dundee and world light-heavyweight champion Willie Pastrano. Dundee remembered the young kid. When Pastrano and Dundee had been in Louisville in 1957 for a fight they let Clay and his brother, Rudolph, visit their room. "He just started telling us he was gonna do this and do that. He was gonna win the Olympics – which he did – he was gonna win the world title – which he did. They stayed for few hours and we mostly talked about boxing", said Dundee.

On December 27, 1960 Clay won for the second time and his relationship with Dundee started. The trainer accepted $125 a week; a deal that lasted until the second fight with Liston, after which he negotiated a percentage deal.

Clay won 19 fights before he met Liston. Some, like the dull and disastrous television appearance against Alonzo Johnson, were fights that continued to raise questions about his temperament and his punch. "Gaseous Cassius", Budd Schulberg called him. Other writers were not so kind and a spiteful cult of Clay, and then Ali, detractors started. There were some fight reports that defied logic and some that were just plain unfair. Others were racist. With hindsight, the blindness of the men who wrote at the time in the face of such brilliance seems quite astonishing.

In Clay's first New York appearance in 1962 he was dropped by Sonny Banks. He recovered to stop Banks as predicted in round four, but he was on the floor and the cynics laughed. He beat Moore, his old trainer, in 1962 and survived another knockdown when he travelled to London to fight Henry Cooper. Cooper's manager, Jim Wicks, responded to a suggestion that Cooper would be meeting Liston in a title fight: "Meeting Liston? I wouldn't let Henry meet him going down the bleedin' street." Wicks and Cooper had more confidence about beating Clay, however.

On that night at Wembley Stadium Clay was criticized for his showmanship. The British press, like most of their American counterparts, simply refused to accept what they were seeing. Instead of concentrating on Clay's skill, they attacked him for his crown and robe outfit.

In round four Clay was down from a left hook when the bell sounded. While Clay was sitting in his corner, Dundee discovered a small tear in the left glove. The timekeeper, Stan Courtney, claimed the break was only one minute 40 seconds between the rounds. The gloves were not replaced, but spares were ready for the end of round five. There was no need, as Cooper was rescued from Clay's fists with lacerations on the left side of his face, and with his left eye a purple mess. The next fight was Liston, and what was for many purists the death of boxing.

Since Floyd Patterson had stopped Moore to win the vacant heavyweight title in 1956 the division had lost a lot of its glamour. Clay was its saviour. Even Liston, who for so long waited patiently as Patterson fought mediocre fighters, seemed intent to just sit and wait for paydays when he beat Patterson. All of Liston's brilliant non-title victories in 1959 and 1960 should have been title defences.

The middleweight, welterweight and, at the end of the 1960s, the light-heavyweight divisions had some of the greats in action against each other. Emile Griffith, Dick Tiger, Bob Foster, Jose Napoles and Carlos Monzon all came through as Gene Fullmer, Paul Pender, Jose Torres and Joey Giardello were finishing their careers. The rivalries and competitive fights at this time match any period in boxing history.

By the end of the 1960s it had all gone horribly wrong for Ali. He was out of the ring from March 1967 until October 1970 because as a Muslim he refused to be inducted for the draft and was disowned by the sport's governing bodies. In early 1964, though, nothing else mattered in boxing but the prospect of Sonny Liston silencing Cassius Clay, the Louisville Lip, in Miami. There appeared to be far more at stake than just the heavyweight championship of the world.

▲ **DOWN BUT NOT OUT**
Clay recovered from Cooper's left hook late in round four of their bout at Wembley Stadium in 1963. The bloody fight came to an end in the following round with Cooper being rescued from Clay's fists.

Clay arrived with predictions and taunted the experts

▲ ONE ENCHANTED NIGHT

"Eighth round he'll be dazed, he'll be frustrated, he'll be tired and nervous", predicted Clay before the first Liston fight in 1964. He promised "a total eclipse of the Sonny" and he delivered.

It was the wildest weigh-in ever. Clay was pronounced "scared to death" by Dr Alexander Robbins. Liston looked bored on the eve of his second defence of his title against the "thunderjaw" who had been stalking and annoying him for far too long.

The fight was in Miami on February 25, 1964. Clay was just 22 and Liston was mean and malevolent. Liston's age was not expected to be a factor but when it was over he suddenly looked older than his years. Nobody really knew exactly how old he was, although his daughter was 17.

Clay played with him. It's that simple. Liston refused to come out of his corner for round seven and Clay was the new heavyweight champion.

"I'm still pretty, the prettiest man alive. But go look at that Liston. He's gone to hospital with his face all cut. Don't ever call me an underdog again. I'm the greatest champ who ever lived. I cut him to pieces", said a jubilant Clay.

Liston claimed to have injured his shoulder, but few believed him. He looked like a man with a shattered soul that night as he sat forlornly in his corner. He must have known there was nothing he could do.

The next morning Clay became Cassius X Clay, and announced his conversion to Islam. At the conference his voice was low. On March 6 he was given the name Muhammad Ali by the leader of the Nation of Islam, Elijah Muhammad.

◀ NO REFUGE FROM THE PAIN

Liston tries to duck below Clay's punches but it was no good. There was no solace for the champ anywhere in the ring.

▲ MOMENTOUS MOMENT

Dundee is all smiles when the news of Liston's injury surrender is known. Clay is the champion, the champion he said he would be.

◀ WHAT HAPPENED?

Joe Louis looks on in stunned confusion. What went wrong? Nobody really knew. "In the ring Sonny was a killing machine. I seen him knock guys out with a jab, just one jab. Bang", said Liston's loyal friend Johnny Tocco.

Ali was one man in a ring paradise creating hell for his opponents

Ali got Patterson in Las Vegas in November 1965. It was arguably the first of his many cruel performances and when it ended in round 12 the public had a clearer picture of the boy from Louisville. "Let's not call this a fight. It was a public humiliation", wrote George Whiting, in the London *Evening Standard*. Ali had promised a sacrifice and he delivered.

After Patterson came the brave Canadian George Chuvalo, in Toronto in 1966. At the same time as the fight was taking place there was a grand jury investigation into Ali's postponed defence against leading contender Ernie Terrell. There were allegations of gangster involvement. Ali would ruin Terrell the following year.

Ali was superb against Chuvalo and won the fight on points. His next three contests were too easy but he had other troubles. The FBI were monitoring him and the spectre of his enlistment in the American forces loomed ever larger.

In London, in May 1966, he cut Henry Cooper again and it was over in round six. In August he was back in London and this time he needed less than three full rounds to knockout Brian London. In September he was in Frankfurt for another defence against southpaw Karl Mildenberger. It went 12 rounds before it was called off. The Mildenberger fight provided a ray of hope for the Ali detractors, who incurred the champion's wrath by still insisting on calling him Clay.

"If he leaves his head open against Cleveland Williams he could be in real trouble", warned Joe Louis. The fight with Williams turned out to be another brutal display. In Europe, Ali had not been so vicious.

◀ **STYLE WAS HIS ANSWER**

Ali fighting German, Karl Mildenberger, in 1966. It was his third easy victory on an obscure and lonely tour of Europe.

▲ AVOIDING EYE CONTACT

Floyd Patterson faces defeat in his 1965 match with Ali. Patterson had a back injury and Ali was cruel – Patterson never stood a chance.

▼ UNLAWFUL CONTACT

Ali and Brian London shake hands before their 1966 fight. The British Board of Boxing Control objected to the fight but it went ahead anyway.

◄ ONE PAINFUL NIGHT

"I could hit him, but he could hit me and he hit me more than I hit him, and I tell ya, whoever said he can't hit was telling a lie', said London after his fight with Ali.

▶ **PROVING A POINT**
Ali points out that he is not the only one opposed to the Vietnam war. His refusal to be inducted into the army was controversial and cost him his licence to box.

Ali knew he was running out of time and running into trouble

Terrell was nicknamed The Octopus by Ali. His style was not easy on the eye but he had beaten Eddie Machen, Zora Folley, Cleveland Williams, George Chuvalo and Doug Jones, a fighter who had given the young Clay a few problems. He was also the World Boxing Association champion and had a jab like a piston.

Before the fight Ali dropped the octopus sobriquet and started to call Terrell Uncle Tom. "What's my name?" Ali began asking before the fight and continued asking during as the two men fought. Terrell always answered: "Cassius Clay."

The action was truly grisly and Terrell was made to suffer for 15 rounds. He took one of modern boxing's most damaging and soul-destroying beatings. Vicious punches altered his face and in his ear he heard the same questioning taunt: "What's my name, what's my name?" There was no twinkle in Ali's eye that night. It was Ali at his most savage.

Terrell claimed Ali had thumbed him in the eye and raked his eyes on a rope but he could do nothing to halt the punches, the taunts and the sneers. At the start of round 13 Ali spat contemptuously at Terrell's feet. When it was over, there were no friendly handshakes. "I made it a great fight with a dull man", boasted the champion.

There would be just one more fight before the government beat him. On March 6, 1967, the National Selective Service Presidential Appeal Board voted unanimously to maintain Ali's 1-A classification. He was officially eligible for induction to the armed forces. As a Muslim he refused, as a black American he refused. "I ain't got no quarrel with them Vietcong", he famously said.

He was due to meet Folley at Madison Square Garden on March 22, but he was rapidly running out of time and had few allies.

◄ **NASTY FROM THE START**

Ali against Terrell in Houston, Texas, in 1967. Ali was at his spiteful best in front of the 37,321 fans. "What's my name", Ali demanded. "Clay", Terrell kept foolishly replying.

▲ **ALI THE PREACHER**

Ali preaches as the guest minister at Frankfurt's Mosque in September 1966. "I believe in Allah and in Peace", said Ali after the first Liston fight.

► **TERRELL ACCUSES ALI**

Terrell blocks a right from Ali. Terrell claimed that Ali thumbed him in the eye and raked his eyes across the ropes. When it was over Ali was treated with indifference by the fans and not admiration.

RUBIN "HURRICANE" CARTER

One Boxer's Hellish Nightmare

he Rubin "Hurricane" Carter story is a tragedy. In 1967 Carter was wrongfully convicted of a triple murder in New Jersey and sentenced to three life terms in prison. Carter was one of the most ferocious boxers in the world. "I think I hold some sort of record for knocking people out of the ring", joked Carter, who always entered the ring wearing a black hooded gown to conceal his shaven head. "He was bad before bad was good", remembers top trainer George Benton.

In 1963, Carter knocked out Emile Griffith but was outpointed by Joey Giardello in a title fight in 1964. The fight with Giardello was delayed and switched from Las Vegas to Philadelphia. There was no disputing the points loss. "I had a bad night", conceded Carter. The first round knock out of Griffith was different. It remains one of only two stoppages in Griffith's career total of 112 fights. "I told Emile to be careful because I knew Rubin could punch but Emile got carried away, listened to Rocky Graziano, and went and got knocked flat with a right", remembers Griffith's loyal trainer Gil Clancy.

Carter entered his living hell on the night of June 16 when he parked his distinctive white Dodge outside the Nite Spot in Paterson, New Jersey. Twelve blocks away, at the Lafayette Bar and Grill, two customers and the barman were brutally murdered at about the same time. Carter had not been in the Lafayette, but was stopped as he drove home from the Nite Spot with John Artis, a young track star. The police were looking for two black men in a white car and they fitted the description.

"I thought it was just harassment. They told us to follow them. We did. There were several cars and the police were leaning out through the windows with shotguns pointing at us. We drove to a bar, a bar I'd never even heard of. They told us to get out. There were a lot of people crying and standing around and I started to get a bad feeling. It was like a lynching", remembered Carter.

It was just the start of Carter's problems, the first steps that would lead to him spending nearly 20 years in prison. Carter and Artis were convicted of the crimes. It was a travesty from the start.

"I was isolated a long time before the murders. In 1964 I spoke out after the Harlem fruit riots, when New York police killed a little black child, and I spoke out and said black people ought to have died in the street protecting their children. Instead they were forced to watch by police holding guns on them as the children were shot. On June 17, 1966, they finally put the handles on me", said Carter. There had been negotiations for Carter to challenge Dick Tiger for the middleweight title in early 1966 and 10 days before the murders took place, Griffith had beaten Tiger for the championship.

In March 1976 Carter and Artis were released on bail after a campaign for their freedom. Ali picked Carter up from Trenton State Prison, but on December 22 Carter and Artis were reconvicted.

Artis was released in 1981 and Carter in November 1985. There was no bail. The game was over for the New Jersey officials. In August 1987 the original conviction was thrown out by United States Supreme Court of Appeals. However, it was not until February 1988 that a judge in Passaic county formally dismissed the indictments. Carter has never received a cent in compensation, or an apology. To this day he will not even fly over New Jersey. He left for Canada in March 1988, a free man, and still lives in Toronto.

▲ **SINGING FOR THE HURRICANE**
Bob Dylan and Joan Baez perform at a benefit evening to raise funds for the release of Carter and John Artis in 1975. Ali was another strong supporter of Carter.

▲ **A MEAN FIGHTER** *"There was a way that I did things back then that was different … I went to the ring with the bad intentions of an angry man."*

Folley was a shadow that Ali left floating on the canvas

▲ THE LAST FIGHT

Ali knew that beating Folley was not his real problem. He won in round seven with a perfect right that stunned the veteran's senses.

Ali had the war in Vietnam on his mind when he sent Zora Folley into oblivion in round seven in front of nearly 14,000 people at Madison Square Garden. The date was March 22, 1967 and Ali would not fight again until October 1970.

He embraced Folley at the end. He liked the veteran. "I don't remember much about the last round, but I don't have to be ashamed at being beaten by a man like Clay – I mean Muhammad Ali", said Folley.

On April 28, 1967, Ali arrived for induction in Houston. He refused to step forward on religious grounds. On May 8 he was indicted by a federal grand jury in Houston and released on $5,000 bail on the condition that he did not leave the United States. In June 1967 the New York State Athletic Commission suspended his licence to box. Other commissions followed. Muhammad Ali was still champion, but there was not a ring for him to fight in.

After refusing to be inducted, Ali gave the media a statement that ended: "There is an alternative, and that alternative is justice. If justice prevails, if my constitutional rights are upheld, I will be forced to go neither to the Army nor jail. In the end, I am confident that justice will come my way, for the truth must eventually prevail."

◄ **GYM PERFECT**

Ali skips in training under the watchful eye of Angelo Dundee. "When Muhammad was in the gym he concentrated on the job. He could still talk, boy could he talk, but he worked and worked", said Dundee. Most training sessions were attended by the press and other members of the public.

▲ **A FOCUSED FIGHTER**

Ali in training. "Ali is quicker than Marciano, hits as hard as Patterson. All he needs now is a little more brain behind his punches", said Archie Moore in 1963.

▶ **A VICTIM OF WAR**

Ali acknowledges his fans as he arrives at the Army Induction Center in Houston. He never went to war and he never went to prison, but he did lose what could have been his finest years as a boxer.

▲ **THE LAST WARNING**

Ali meets with the press at Orly Airport in Paris en route for his fight with George Foreman in Zaire. "You better listen to what I say", he warned. Behind him Don King was laughing.

◄ **COOL DAYS FOR ALI**

Previous page: The victorious champion relaxes after beating his arch rival Joe Frazier in January 1974.

Muhammad Ali lost to Joe Frazier and George Foreman beat Frazier, but he couldn't beat Ali. "I kept telling him he had no punch, he swings like a sissy and then I knocked him out. I told you all I would and you never listened", said Ali. He was right, few people listened or believed.

FOREVER KINGS

Times changed. After Muhammad Ali returned to the ring against Jerry Quarry in 1970 he met Oscar Bonavena. Ali won both fights but it was a different Ali – a stronger, slower, wiser Ali. Was he better? Critics and fans remain divided. Angelo Dundee maintains that the best of Ali was lost in his three and a half year exile. It makes no difference, because by late 1970 Joe Frazier was the champion and he was clearly more than just a temporary resident.

Ali and Frazier was a natural fight to make. The pair met at Madison Square Garden in March 1971, in a fight that would forever change the position of boxing in society. It was more than just the first heavyweight championship meeting between two unbeaten fighters – it was dubbed The Fight of the Century. Ali's taunting of Frazier helped create the scene.

There was only one winner in the ring on that night and it was Smokin' Joe, but after Ali lifted

himself up from the knockdown in the last round he went on to create boxing history again and again. Part of that history would see him go on to beat Frazier on two occasions.

"I couldn't be what I am without him and he couldn't be what he is without me", said Ali, after beating Frazier in the Thrilla' in Manila in 1975. The fight was arguably the best heavyweight bout in boxing's history. It was also the last great performance by either man.

Even before Ali and Frazier fought for the first time, the presence of George Foreman on boxing's horizon proved an ominous sight. The young Foreman, who jabbed and smashed his way past George Chuvalo in 1970, was one of the best heavyweight prospects ever. His jab, a feature of his boxing style so often overlooked by commentators, ruined Chuvalo.

Foreman won the title in 1973 and his raw power came to rule the division and dominate the sport, until one night in the jungles of Zaire, when Ali beat him and became the Greatest. When Foreman won and again when he lost, Donald King was right there – the best-known unknown, unattached at the time but connected to everybody.

In addition to Foreman, there were other fighters like Jerry Quarry, Earnie Shavers and Ken Norton waiting for their chance. In the late 1970s Larry Holmes, a former Ali sparring partner, and the unfortunate Neon Leon Spinks emerged on the scene. The 1970s was heavyweight boxing's greatest decade.

The 12 top heavyweights that were fighting at the start of the 1980s were talented but, like Neon Leon, many wasted their talents and several ended up addicted to cocaine. They were a lost generation of fighters and a brutal contrast to the men who will remain champions forever. Holmes, who started fighting under the nickname Black Cloud, was the glorious exception and belongs in the company of Frazier, Foreman and Ali.

The heavyweights came close to eclipsing the other weights in the 1970s but the quality of the champions in all divisions was so good that not even Ali could overshadow all the other greats. From Bob Foster all the way down to the fearsome Z-men – Carlos Zarate and Alfonso Zamora – the 1970s produced some of the best pound-for-pound fighters in history. Jose Napoles, Antonio Cervantes, Wilfredo Gomez, Carlos Monzon, Ruben Olivares, Alexis Arguello, Wilfred Benitez and Roberto Duran all won titles during a decade of brilliance. By 1979 Sugar Ray Leonard had won his first title. It was Leonard and his opponents who would shape the next decade.

One fight in 1977 is a perfect example of the type of quality fighter that was around towards the end of the 1970s. In April, Carlos Zarate, the WBC bantamweight champion, met another Mexican, Alfonso Zamora, who held the WBA version, in Los Angeles. Zarate was unbeaten in 38 fights with 37 stoppages and Zamora had a perfect record of 29 wins with 29 stoppages or knockouts. There were no titles up for stake, just too much pride and the fight was made two pounds above the limit. Zarate won in four. Zamora was never the same again and lost his title in his next fight. Zarate was stopped the following year when he challenged Wilfredo Gomez for the WBC super-bantamweight title.

The saddest event of the 1970s was undoubtedly

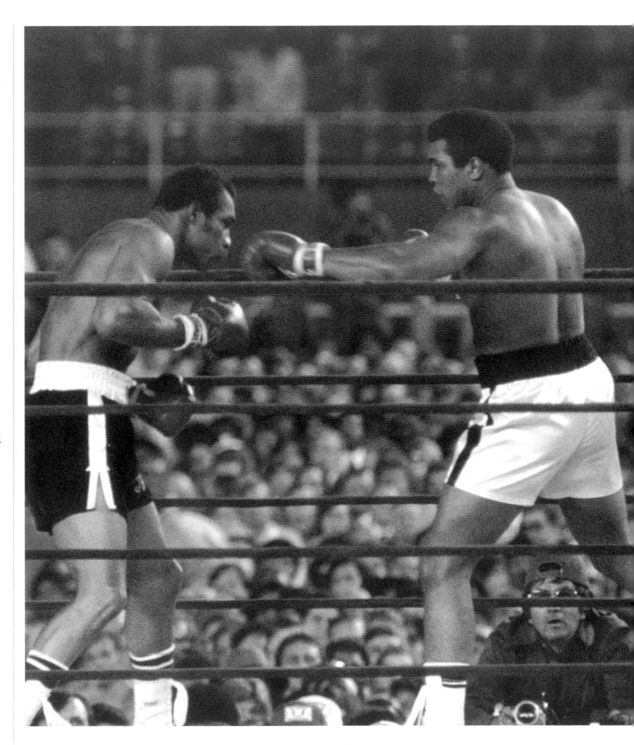

the death of Sonny Liston in January 1971. He had been dead for several days before he was found in his Las Vegas apartment. Police reports said there was heroin on a kitchen table and needle marks in his arm. It was the end that many people expected, but loyal friends denied it was self-inflicted. "Sonny hated needles. He never killed himself", insisted Johnny Tocco, the Las Vegas trainer whose gym became one of the most famous in the world. His death is still a mystery. Liston is buried out by the airport in Las Vegas, his simple plot a scene of regular homage.

▲ **A TOUGH FIGHTER**
Ali had trouble with Ken Norton. They met three times, went 39 rounds and every round was tight. "I knew what to do and I never listened to his mouth", said Norton.

Other great fighters were ignored because of Ali, Foreman and Frazier

In late 1970 Jose Napoles briefly lost his welterweight title to Billy Backus because of a cut eye. When he won it back in the 1971 rematch, Backus's face was so badly swollen the doctor called the fight off. Napoles had a knack of making his punches look light when in reality they were powerful and accurate.

Napoles decided to step up in weight and fight Monzon for the middleweight title in 1974. It was risky, but it was a fight that he could possibly have won. Monzon was untouchable and stopped the Cuban-born fighter at the end of round six.

When Napoles finally lost his welterweight title to London's John H. Stracey in 1975 it was in Mexico City, where he had lived since leaving his wife and small baby in Cuba in 1961. In his two reigns as champion he made 13 defences, including one against Emile Griffith, and ranks as one of the best welterweights in boxing's history. Just a few years earlier or a few years later and Napoles would have undoubtedly proved his class in a division that was in a slump during his peak.

Like Ken Buchanan and light-heavyweight champion John Conteh, whose career is one of the tragedies of modern British boxing, Stracey ended his boxing life with little more than memories from his moment of glory. His win over Napoles is one of the best ever by a British fighter, even if the champion was at the end of a great career.

▶ **A BAD END**

John Conteh swings a right at Joe Cokes. Before Conteh won the world light-heavyweight title he acted like he was determined to wreck his career and ruin his life. "I did some stupid things, but had some great times", he said.

◀ THE SAD BOXER

Jose Napoles looks subdued, despite having just won the world title. Napoles had to leave behind his wife and child in Cuba and move to Mexico to continue his boxing career.

▼ A MEAN RECORD

Carlos Monzon never missed a beat in the ring. He lost just three times in 101 fights over a 14-year period.

▲ THE BULLRING STUNT

John H. Stracey took the welterweight title from Napoles in Mexico City in 1975. "I could hear the people chanting his name before I saw them. The fight was in a bullring and the fans had come to see Napoles tame me. They left unhappy, I'm pleased to say", commented Stracey.

Leonard and the Spinks brothers made Montreal magic

▲ **THE FINAL GOLD**

Sugar Ray Leonard – seen here beating Valery Limasov of the Soviet Union at the 1976 Montreal Olympics – was the man many thought would replace Muhammad Ali. Within two years of winning the light-welterweight gold at Montreal, Leonard had fought on all the major TV channels and was rapidly becoming a star attraction.

For Americans, the Olympic ring has never been as blessed as it was in Montreal in 1976. It was the year Sugar Ray Leonard, and Michael and Leon Spinks won gold. It was also the last year the US beat Cuba.

In the finals four Americans beat Cubans in fights that went far beyond the usual importance of the event. The light-heavyweight final between a weary Leon Spinks and Cuba's Sixto Soria was one of the most exciting in Olympic history. In addition to the Spinks brothers and Leonard, flyweight Leo Randolph and lightweight Howard Davis also won gold. Cuba still had three gold winners, including Stevenson.

In 1978 when Soria won the world championship, his former opponent Leon Spinks was the heavyweight champion of the world, having outpointed Ali in February 1978. By the time Soria was back in Havana in late May, his future secure, Spinks was on a self-destruct mission. Ali won their rematch in September 1978 but Neon Leon had lost his way in the champagne haze that had begun to shroud his chaotic life.

Watching Stevenson perform his duties as a sporting ambassador at the 1996 Olympics and then catching a glimpse of Leon Spinks, his face an expressionless mask, at ringside when Lennox Lewis, another Olympic champion, defended his WBC heavyweight title against Andrew Golota, in October 1997, was a harsh reminder of professional boxing's cruel tendencies. In 1978 it was oh so different.

▲ AN UNEXPECTED VICTORY

Cuba's Sixto Soria is knocked down by Leon Spinks in the 1976 final for the heavyweight gold medal. Soria was brilliant and Spinks was expected to lose. "I heard he was the man and that just made me wanna do the thing. I had him hurt and I never stopped hurting him. I forgot how tired I was, I just wanted to hear 'Leon Spinks Olympic champion' ", said Spinks later.

MILESTONES OF BOXING

• • • • • • • • • • • • • • • •

ALI'S THIRD CHAMPIONSHIP WIN

Muhammad Ali made history by winning the heavyweight championship for the third time in his rematch with Leon Spinks in 1978. "I did it before and now I have done it again. Against Liston you said no, against Foreman you said no and against Spinks you said 'The champ's too old', well I done it and I might just do it again", said Ali.

It is possible, however, that at this time Ali was not the best heavyweight in the world. Larry Holmes had won the title three months earlier when he beat Norton. "I knew I could have beaten him then but how could I shout my mouth off. He was my idol and I just had to wait and see what happened", claimed Holmes.

Ali was back in the ring to try and "do it again" in 1980. He failed, when in one of sport's great tragedies, he was easily stopped by Holmes.

Holmes stays on top as the new boys begin to emerge

▲ A STORM IN THE PALACE

When Holmes fought Norton at Caesars Palace in Las Vegas the crowd witnessed one of the best fights of the 1970s. Holmes won and held the title for seven years.

Larry Holmes beat Ken Norton to become the WBC heavyweight champion in 1978. Holmes was still fighting for versions of the heavyweight title 19 years later, a relic from a previous time, a survivor of the decade when champions were forever. He was as remarkable back in 1978 as he is now.

Marvelous Marvin Hagler was like Holmes. Neither were glamour fighters. When Hagler declared 'I'm black, I'm a southpaw and I'm good', he was acknowledging a debt to Ali. It was Ali that had helped give all fighters a voice, even if sometimes his own fell silent when he should have been able to simply say "No".

Hagler drew with Vito Antuofermo for the undisputed middleweight title in 1979. It was just another setback for the Marvelous one, who would win the title from Alan Minter in 1980 in London, in a fight sadly remembered more for the mindless violence of the crowd, than the boxing.

It was also in 1979 that Sugar Ray Leonard, the Olympic golden boy, won his first title when he stopped Wilfred Benitez in round 15 to win the WBC welterweight championship.

Duran was looking for more titles, and Tommy Hearns, a tall skinny kid with a sweet right cross, was starting to make people watch. The new-look boxing scene had Hagler, Duran, Leonard and Hearns and Las Vegas wanted them bad.

◀ **SO NEAR SO OFTEN**

Ken Norton could always be relied upon to put up a tough battle – the fight with Holmes in 1978 was perfect example. Norton had also beaten Ali in 1973 when he broke Ali's jaw, but he lost the rematch the same year.

▲ **A TRUE CHAMPION**

Larry Holmes shows off his belt at a press conference in London in 1978. Holmes was a great heavyweight but coming in the middle of two such larger-than-life characters like Ali and Tyson meant he never gained the recognition he deserved.

The
VEGAS
boys

1980-1986

▶ **THE BIG DAY APPROACHES**

Hearns and Duran step up the pre-fight hype. On the day, Hearns knocked Duran out. The stage was set for the Hearns-Hagler bout. "If I get the right clean on Hagler he is going down", promised Hearns.

Pride was at stake in each of the furious meetings in the Nevada heat

▲ **MARVELOUS MARVIN**

"There is a monster that comes out when I'm in the ring. I think it goes back to the days when I had nothing. They're all trying to take something from me that I have worked long and hard for", Hagler once commented.

Marvelous Marvin Hagler lacked the glamour of Sugar Ray Leonard and Tommy Hearns. He knew it, but it didn't seem to bother him when he first won the middleweight title. The resentment increased, however, as the years passed. "Marvin just did what he had to do", said Goody Petronelli, his trainer. No thrills, just raw power and determination.

After seven defences Hagler was matched with one of his idols, Roberto Duran, in Las Vegas in 1983. It was close and after 13 rounds all three judges had Duran in front. But Hagler was familiar with adversity and reached deep inside, at Petronelli's urging, to find enough in reserve to win the 14th and 15th rounds. His title was safe and he won a split decision.

He had won with old-fashioned skills, not the techniques used by Leonard to beat Duran in 1980. There was talk after Hagler beat Duran that a fight with Leonard would be next. The talk continued until 1987 when they finally met.

In 1984 Hearns knocked out Duran to provide Hagler with an alternative. "When Tommy nailed him, he was jabbing the body, all part of setting Duran up. With Duran concentrating on the body, Tommy dropped over the right and knocked him out", explained Steward. It was perfect, too perfect for Hagler to accept without a response.

Hagler against Hearns for the undisputed middleweight championship, which was known simply as The Fight, was made for Monday, April 15, 1985. Caesars Palace, Las Vegas, was once again the venue.

◀ DURAN V HAGLER

Duran throws a left at Hagler during their 1983 fight. It went 15 rounds, with Duran losing on points. Duran was Hagler's idol. The fight was close until Hagler's late burst. "If Marvin had put the pressure on in the first 10 rounds it would not have gone 15 rounds", said Goody Petronelli.

MILESTONES OF BOXING

• • • • • • • • • • • • • • • •

MONEY, VEGAS AND BOXING

In the early 1980s the city known as Lost Wages was established as boxing's latest resort – a showcase city for the excesses of the sport. The casinos make the fights happen by paying large site fees – the money is returned when the pit drop increases.

Caesars, the Hilton and, in the 1990s, the MGM are the names fight fans know. They have replaced the American ballparks and Madison Square Garden as the venues for famous fights.

Some of boxing's modern classics have taken place in Vegas. Most of the fights between Hagler, Hearns, Duran and Leonard and the complicated series of heavyweight title fights that followed the demise of Ali, for instance, have been staged there.

The dominance of Vegas as a boxing mecca is evident by the fact that there are more current or former boxers living in the city than anywhere else. Some are wealthy, some are struggling and many are on the poverty line. Las Vegas is an easy place for boxing's winners, but there are few of them.

Tyson was the pride of D'Amato and they were boxing's immediate future

The man in the shadows during the mid-1980s was Mike Tyson. He was there in 1985 as the heavyweight title changed hands, and while many fighters were in a state of flux, he was slowly making his way to the top.

In April 1986, Larry Holmes lost a disputed split decision to Michael Spinks. "It's over. This is it. I know I can't win no more. There's no sense in chasing ghosts. It hurts because I worked so hard. I sacrificed so much" said Holmes. But he came back.

Spinks was gracious in victory: "Larry was fighting for his life. He fought to the very end." However, Spinks was looking over his shoulder at Tyson, the man-child from Cus D'Amato's Catskill retreat.

In March 1986 Trevor Berbick, a constant traveller in the heavyweight zone, finally won the title when he beat Pinklon Thomas.

In New York and New Jersey, Tyson kept winning. All of Tyson's opponents were the right men for the job. Many were part of the legion of sparring partners and hired-hands that so many heavyweights belong to. They talked, and a sense of fear developed. There was something disturbing about the kid from Brooklyn and his odd group. Don King worked hard in late 1985 to get as close as possible to Tyson.

In November 1986 Tyson met Berbick for the WBC title. The fight was in Las Vegas, where 17 of the previous 34 world title fights had been staged. The sport was one short fight away from a glorious future. Sadly, Tyson was just a few years away from a hell of his own making, but in the weeks before the Berbick fight the 20-year-old boxer was pure.

◀ **FAIRYTALE BOY**
Tyson devastated his opponents.
"Cus taught me. I owe it all to
Cus", Tyson insisted. Others blamed
D'Amato for Tyson's frailties outside
the ring – nobody doubted the
influence of the sage from the New
York woods on Tyson in the ring.

▶ THE OTHER BROTHER

Michael Spinks kept his head, stayed in control and retained his money. "I told Leon that the people around him were trying to turn him against his family. I had different people next to me", Michael said.

▲ SPINKS WINS THROUGH

Larry Holmes backs away from Michael Spinks in the second round of their 1985 title fight in Las Vegas. Spinks defeated Holmes to take the heavyweight title.

◀ GRUDGE MATCH

Tyson and Mitch Green go 10 rounds in 1986. "Mitch Green was always talking nonsense and saying this and that. I wanted to make his suffer slow", Tyson said. The pair later had a fight outside an all-night tailor's shop in Harlem. Tyson won again.

197

The
NEW
bad boy

1986-1994

The awesome power of Mike Tyson was first unveiled in 1985. A poor kid from Brooklyn, Tyson lived for boxing and was poised to become the greatest champion in the sport's history.

D'AMATO'S BABE TURNS SOUR

▲ STATEMENT OF INTENT

"I refuse to lose in the ring", said Tyson after beating Mitch Green in 1986. At the time he looked untouchable, and there were seemingly a string of fighters waiting in line to be sacrificed.

◄ "RAZOR" IS BLUNTED!

Previous page: Tyson launches a ferocious right hand at Ruddock during the first of their two fights.

In November 1985 Cus D'Amato died. He left behind his last offering to the sport of boxing, a boxer once so pure and perfect that D'Amato's suggestion that Mike Tyson would be the greatest fighter in history appeared possible.

Tyson was born poor in Brooklyn. He was also born bad and after several scrapes with the law was placed at the age of 13 in the Tryon School for boys in upstate New York. He was nearly 200 pounds, just five foot eight and had an incongruous, high-pitched voice. In Brownsville he was known as Big Head Mike or Little Fairy Boy.

At Tryon Tyson came under the influence of former pro Bobby Stewart. The pair worked together in the gym and in 1980 Stewart made contact with D'Amato. In March 1980, at D'Amato's gym, the trainer watched three rounds of Tyson sparring with Stewart and stated: "That's the heavyweight champion of the world." On June 30, 1980, Tyson was released into D'Amato's custody. He had a legal guardian and a future in the boxing ring.

The troubles did not come to a stop when Tyson left Tryon, however. They never came to a stop. D'Amato concentrated on curbing Tyson's emotions in the ring but ignored his dangerous behaviour outside it. The product became too important and indiscretions were overlooked and excused. Unfortunately, Tyson's boxing education failed to include valuable lessons in distinguishing between right and wrong.

In May 1985 Tyson turned professional after 35 amateur contests and a further 19 fights in amateur "smokers". The opponents started to fall. The men from the list of reliable losers made their money in brief and painful encounters with boxing's young star. The news spread as word started to filter through from survivors of undercard beatings. The heavyweight scene was in waiting as Tyson knocked men over and out.

In 1985 Tyson fought 15 times and stopped those 15 opponents in a total of just 22 rounds – 11 went in round one. Some of the beaten men had reputations for losing in style but Tyson ruined them. By the end of 1985 he was being watched and not just by the heavyweights on the championship merry-go-round. There were others with plans.

Tyson's first fight for Don King was in May 1986, against former New York gang leader Mitch "Blood" Green in Madison Square Garden. It went 10 rounds. Two years later Tyson and Green had another fight, again in New York – at four in the morning outside a tailor's shop in Harlem. According to eyewitnesses, Tyson won the rematch.

The last fight in 1986 was against Trevor Berbick for the WBC heavyweight championship. King was the promoter, but Tyson was still managed by Jim Jacobs and his partner Bill Cayton, who at the time did not have a boxing manager's licence. Cayton and Jacobs had invited King in. The struggle over Tyson's future guidance was inevitable and, according to Tyson's trainer, and one of D'Amato's loyal boys, Kevin Rooney, the problem was King. "He hung around like a dog", said Rooney.

Before the fight Berbick was not intimidated. "Tyson is just a one-way fighter. He doesn't have a good jab and he is not a smart fighter. I will back him up." He tried but he was overwhelmed. It ended in round two and 20-year-old Tyson was the youngest heavyweight champion of the world.

The heavyweights were now in trouble.

First to go was James "Bonecrusher" Smith, but the fight lasted 12 rounds. Smith was sensible enough to survive but Tyson won the WBA belt. Next, in May 1987, was Pinklon Thomas, the former champion. It went six rounds and Tyson retained both titles. Before the fight Thomas used a line that Evander Holyfield repeated in 1996 and 1997. "He comes from the same mean streets as me. I seen the same things", said Thomas.

"Mike has an image. He thought that by having a certain perception it helped him win fights", said D'Amato protege, Teddy Atlas. The image was simple: Tyson had been told he was savage and ruthless by people close to him and tried to uphold that reputation. In a lot of his fights the image worked, and his opponents' fear helped him.

In August 1987 Tyson unified the titles by beating Tony Tucker for the IBF belt. It went 12 rounds. Tyson was the new unified champion of the world.
In late 1987 he made the first of six defences of the unified world title and stopped Tyrell Biggs, the 1984 Olympic super-heavyweight champion, in seven rounds. Tyson had disliked Biggs since before the Olympics when the two had sparred.

It may have been a great year in the ring for Tyson, but his life away from boxing was starting to come apart. By the start of 1988 Michael Gerard Tyson's life had changed – by the end of the traumatic year the signs of destruction were already clear.

▼ **FINAL TITLE SAFE**
Tony Tucker went 12 rounds and had the right idea against Tyson in August 1987, but when it was over Tyson had the IBF, WBA and WBC belts. He was midway through his prime first period as champion.

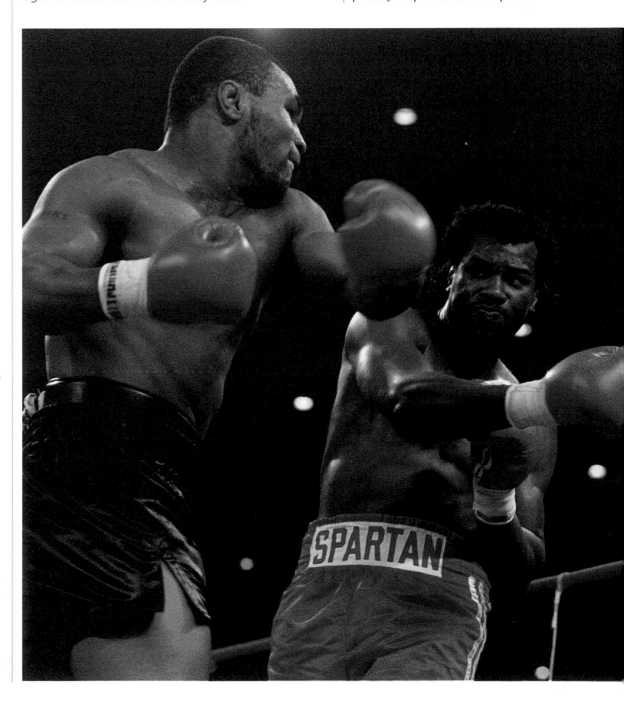

Tyson's destruction of Spinks instilled fear in the division

In March 1988 Tyson lost his mentor Jim Jacobs. It was a shock, nobody had told the fighter that Jacobs was ill! Tyson gained a wife in Robin Givens but their sad marriage was over by October and in November his dispute with Cayton intensified. Rooney was also gone by the end of the year. King was in the background offering promotional agreements. It was a horrible time for the fighter.

In the ring that year Tyson took care of business with three wins, but there were many watching who saw the obvious changes. Tyson was slack.

In January 1988 he had stopped Larry Holmes in round four. Holmes had the right idea but Tyson, after a severe reprimand from Rooney at the end of round two – possibly the last time a cornerman dared criticize Tyson during a fight – returned to his old style and the speed was too much for Holmes. The ending was as savage as any of Tyson's knockout wins.

In March 1988 Tyson took his new bride to Tokyo, where he stopped former champion Tony Tubbs in two rounds. Two days later, after Tyson had returned to New York, he was told that Jacobs was dead. King used the funeral in Los Angeles as an opportunity to move even closer to the fighter.

By the time Tyson knocked out Michael Spinks in June of the same year his relationship with Cayton was in turmoil and his marriage was a sham. Because of the circumstances Spinks had an opportunity. Tyson, however, overcame the pressures to ruin Spinks in just 91 seconds.

◄ **SPINKS'S DELUSION**
Michael Spinks was utterly destroyed in 91 seconds of his fight with Tyson, in June 1988, but after the contest he was in reflective mood. "I thought there was a way to beat him, I still do. On the night it went wrong and he took me out. That is what can happen in boxing."

▲ PRIMED FOR A FALL

An early studio shot of Tyson in his prime, but there were already signs of trouble. During 1988, several acts of careless behaviour dominated his life outside the ropes.

▶ END FOR THE CITY MAN

"Each day I would meet with Jim (Jacobs) to discuss what to do with Mike", said Cayton. However, when Jacobs died in March 1988, Cayton was running out of time and Don King was looming large.

▼ THE OLD MAN IS BACK

"I don't want to hear about age and don't tell me how good Tyson is. I know what I'm doing", said Larry Holmes before his fight with Tyson in January 1988. Holmes was easily beaten in four rounds.

▲ D'AMATO MAN OUSTED

Kevin Rooney was instructed in the ways of boxing and fear by Cus D'Amato. He was the man Tyson trusted and needed in the corner, but their relationship was soured when Tyson married Robin Givens. "Mike lost control", claimed Rooney.

203

The British flags stopped waving as Tyson ruined Bruno in five rounds

▶ **ANOTHER SAD NIGHT**

Bruno throws a left jab at Tyson early in the fight. At one point he managed to hurt the champion with a left hook but in the end there was little for the British fans to cheer about. After the fight, Tyson was in dismissive mood. "How dare they challenge me with their primitive skills. I feel sorry for the guys who want to fight me."

Tyson was out of the ring for eight months before he defended against Frank Bruno in February 1989. The fight had been postponed five times and Tyson had watched as his life changed dramatically in a crazily short period of time. By February 1989 Givens, Rooney and Jacobs were gone forever. King, the "Only in America" man, was in charge.

Tyson left Bruno a wrecked shell on the ropes in round five, but in the first round was caught and clearly hurt by a left hook. The single punch was enough to confirm the worst for the Tyson-watchers. In reality fighting was the easiest part of Tyson's life. It may well have been before, and certainly has been ever since.

In 1989 the ring was still a noble retreat for Tyson, a place of violent sanctuary.

In July he stopped Carl "The Truth" Williams in one round. Williams had a plan and like Biggs had sparred with Tyson. It lasted 93 seconds. If Tyson was having trouble in his private life and his reflexes, punches and feet were slowing down, as many claimed, he was still too much for any of his peers.

The lost generation of heavyweights were deep into their declines. George Foreman had just returned after a 10-year absence, Holyfield was not yet big enough and Riddick Bowe and Lennox Lewis were novices. By the end of 1989 the only person Tyson had to lose to was himself.

▲ **BRUNO UNDER FIRE**

Bruno tries to duck from a barrage of punches in the first round. "I was too stiff, too nervous and just froze when he caught me. We were in Vegas and the pressure was starting to get to me", Bruno offered as explanation. Seven years later Bruno returned to the city of the slaughter and was mauled once again by Tyson.

◄ **A MAN IN TROUBLE**

Bruno receives a count from the referee after a first-round knockdown. Although Tyson destroyed Bruno, he met with his critics after the fight and furiously denied suggestions that his time was running out. However, after one more quick win he went to Tokyo and lost for the first time in his professional career.

TYSON v DOUGLAS

Fantasy Night in Tokyo for Buster

▼ **DOOM IN NEON CITY**

Tyson's turbulent life outside the ropes finally caught up with him as he groped for his gumshield on the canvas in round 10. Douglas, the underdog, had won. "I just want to get back in the ring. Losing is part of the business", said a resolute Tyson at the fight's end.

The final fight of Mike Tyson's first reign as heavyweight champion ended in diabolical farce, pain and insult.

In February 1990 Tyson was in Tokyo to fight James "Buster" Douglas. It was expected to be easy, with odds set at 40-1 against Douglas winning. In 1987 Douglas had faded and was stopped by Tony Tucker in an IBF title fight. His heart was deemed dubious.

In training Tyson looked awful and was dropped by Greg Page, a former champion. Douglas had beaten Page and there was a suggestion that slow ticket sales inspired the so-called knockdown.

Even if it was a set-up, Tyson was not himself.

"I will just hit him and keep hitting him", promised Douglas. Nobody listened, but there were signs that Douglas was a new man. In recent months he had separated from his wife – the mother of his son, Lamar, had been diagnosed with terminal cancer – and in January 1990 his beloved mother died. He was inspired and fearless, whereas Tyson was bored and listless.

The fight was weird from the start. Tyson was not moving his head or his feet. He was easy to hit and Douglas was hitting him. Tyson's cornermen, Aaron Snowell and Jay Bright, were hopeless as the panic increased and the rounds passed. Douglas was resisting. In round five Tyson's left eye started to swell. In his corner the search for an Enswell, the small piece of curved steel that good cornermen sink in ice and use to move swellings, proved fruitless. In its place a condom was packed with ice and rubbed over the eye. It was that type of corner! The strangeness continued until round eight, when Tyson landed a right to send Douglas down. It was all over, many believed. They were wrong. Douglas smashed the canvas in frustration, was lucid, and climbed up as referee, Octavio Meyran, reached nine. The fight started again, but the bell sounded.

Douglas wanted to win and nothing would stop him. In round nine he sought Tyson out in brutal battle, and when the bell sounded it was obvious that boxing would have a new champion. Tyson was stuck in the centre of the ring, his mind devoid of desire.

In round 10 Tyson walked out to slaughter and was duly butchered. He went down heavily from a left, after right had landed and frozen him upright, but dazed. On the canvas Tyson worked in slow motion to pick up his gumshield. At ringside King was screaming, and as the seconds of the final count passed Tyson was on his feet. However, he could not stand alone and it was waved off. Iron Mike was beaten. Seldom in the history of boxing have so many silent witnesses suddenly stepped forward at a fight's conclusion and declared: "I knew that would happen."

Four hours later Jose Sulaiman and Gilberto Mendoza, the respective presidents of the WBC and the WBA suspended recognition of Douglas because in round eight he had been on the floor longer than 10 seconds. King had led the appeal, but it was an action he would regret. "I knocked him out before he knocked me out", claimed Tyson. Within days everybody was backtracking. "Douglas is the true champion", King said in New York. The WBA and WBC quickly agreed.

In October 1990 Douglas collapsed in round three when Evander Holyfield connected cleanly for the first time. "He could have got up", claimed referee Mills Lane. In Tokyo he could have stayed down, but on that wonderful day he had as much heart and desire as any boxer in the sport's history.

▲ **DOUGLAS THE CHAMP** *"This is the dream" said Douglas. "I knew I could do it, I had the determination to succeed and I whupped his ass!"*

Away from Tyson, carnival fighters like Chavez and Whitaker ruled

▶ CHAVEZ V KAMAU

David Kamau extended Chavez in their WBC light-welterweight title fight in 1995. Chavez won, but his power was starting to diminish after years of training, hard living and weight reduction.

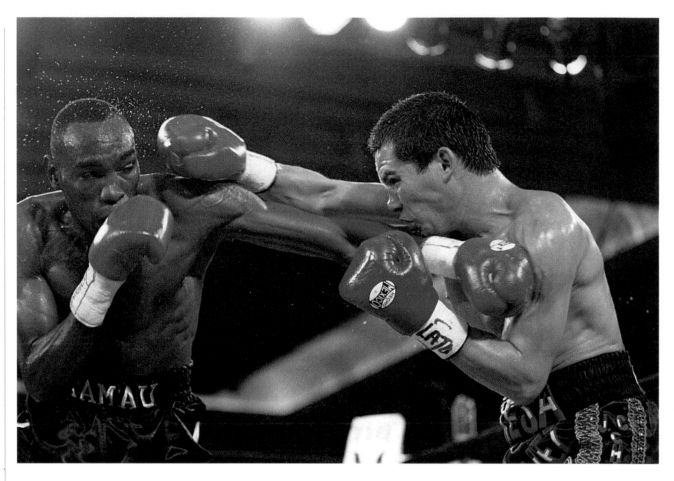

▲ HAPPY WINNER, BAD LOSER

"They say Chavez is unbeatable – that suits me. I have heard he is dirty – that suits me. I know he is a bad loser, and that suits me", said Pernell Whitaker before his controversial draw with the Mexican in 1993. "C'mon, I won clearly", he said when it was all over. He did.

Two fighters from the lower divisions dominated the late 1980s and 1990s: Julio Cesar Chavez, who was blessed with a loyal following and a solid chin, and Pernell Whitaker, a gold medalist in 1984 with a tricky and often ugly southpaw style. Both lacked charisma.

Less than one month after Tyson's fall, Chavez stopped Meldrick Taylor with just two seconds left in the last round to add the IBF junior-welterweight title to his WBC super-lightweight belt.

The Mexican idol was losing on two scorecards and was saved when referee, Richard Steele, intervened. Taylor complained later, but had failed to respond to Steele's questions during the dark moments in the ring. It was Chavez's 69th straight win. His first loss was against Frankie Randall in his 91st fight in 1994, although there were many who believed the first loss was actually in 1993 when Chavez drew with Pernell Whitaker in a challenge for the WBC welterweight title.

In 1994 Chavez beat Randall in a rematch and stopped Taylor in round eight but the Mexican had turned from winner to whiner and was losing respect. In 1996 he was cruelly cut and beaten in four rounds by Oscar De La Hoya.

Whitaker won his first title, the IBF lightweight belt, in 1989 and in the same year avenged a controversial defeat by winning the WBC version from Jose Luis Ramirez. In 1990 he beat Azumah Nelson and then added the WBA version after knocking out Juan Nazario in the first. He won the IBF junior-welter in 1992, the WBC welter in 1993 and in 1995 defied the odds to win the WBA light-middleweight championship. In 1997 De La Hoya won a close and disputed points verdict to take Whitaker's WBC welterweight title.

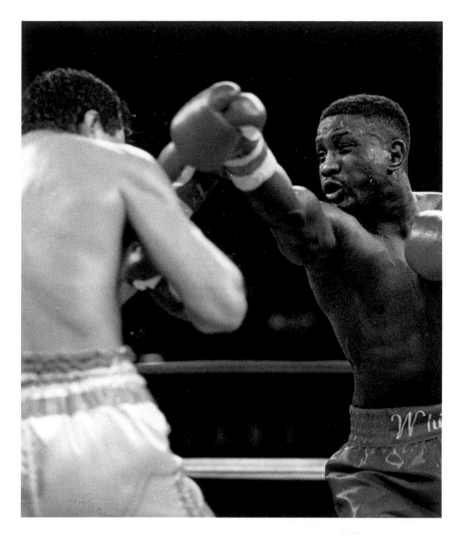

▲ **NO DOUBTERS LEFT**
Whitaker (top) won a title at a fourth weight when he stepped up to light-middleweight to beat WBA champion, Julio Vasquez, in 1995, in another stunning display.

▲ **THE SELF-PROCLAIMED KING**
"When you fight Pernell Whitaker you're not fighting 'Joe Blow' – you're fighting the king", said Whitaker (above) before losing to Oscar De La Hoya in 1997.

MILESTONES OF BOXING
• • • • • • • • • • • • • • • •
MIKE TYSON BEATS TREVOR BERBICK TO WIN WBC HEAVYWEIGHT TITLE
NOVEMBER 22 1986. LAS VEGAS.

Mike Tyson became the youngest heavyweight champion of the world at the age of 20 when he stopped Trevor Berbick to win the WBC title in Las Vegas. He knew he would win, knew he would knock out Berbick, and on the night he dominated.

It was classic Tyson. He rolled with each shot and scored from the angles that he had been taught. Berbick was chopped and rocked from the start and his head quickly lost control of the rest of his body. He was willing, but his bravery hurt him in the end.

For Tyson it was the first step. His mentor, Cus D'Amato, had died a year earlier but he left his legacy of fear in the head of the fighter he had spent so many hours creating. "I couldn't have done this without Cus" Tyson would often say.

In Britain a boxing revolution was led by an unlikely fighter

In Las Vegas, in 1990, Nigel Benn dropped Iran Barkley three times and stopped him after two minutes and 57 seconds of round one. He retained his WBO middleweight title, but it was a bad-tempered brawl and Barkley and his handlers were angry at the former British soldier's abuses. "They are crying like babies" said Benn, "I love stuffing it up Americans."

Benn returned to Britain and agreed terms to defend against Chris Eubank. In America nobody paid much attention to the fight, but a crowd of 9,000 packed the NEC, Birmingham, in November, 1990, and watched one of the best-ever British fights. Eubank won in round nine and a golden period in British boxing started. It coincided with the WBO's efforts to establish themselves. The WBO had Eubank and he was British boxing.

Eubank retained his WBO middleweight title three times, before winning the vacant WBO super-

▲ **BENN SHARES A JOKE**
Nigel Benn with actor, Pierce Brosnan, in jocular mood in Dublin in 1996.

◄ **THE EGO HAS LANDED**
"My aim is to improve the quality of my life and to achieve my goal. I have selected the noble art as a profession." Eubank was a cult attraction from the start.

middleweight title and retaining it 14 times. His earnings were far in excess of the amounts American boxers at the same weight made during the time. The eccentric boxer from Brighton created a new audience for the sport in Britain. Purists and old-timers disliked him from the start, but thousands paid and millions watched him on television.

In 1991, Eubank vacated the WBO middleweight title to avoid a mandatory defence against the dangerous young American Gerald McClellan; and agreed terms for a rematch with Michael Watson, a boxer from London, who had knocked out Benn in 1989. In the first fight with Watson the judges decided that Eubank had done enough to retain his middleweight title. The second fight and its tragic outcome are now part of British boxing lore.

▲ BENN HANGS ON

Benn avoids a lead right from Eubank during their first fight in 1990. "He (Eubank) is an idiot, a con merchant and I will just take him out as quick as possible", said Benn before the fight, but his words came to nothing in round nine.

◄ EUBANK EUPHORIC

A victorious Chris Eubank slowly sinks to his knees in joy, as his beaten foe is consoled by the referee in the background.

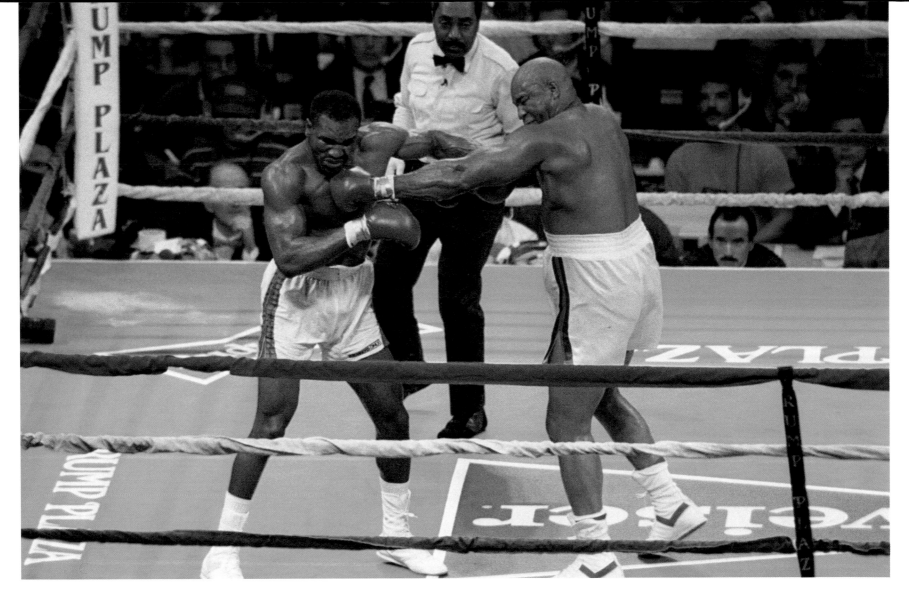

"There is no killer inside anymore" – George Foreman, Tokyo, 1996

▲ **PREACHER STILL HAS IT**

Foreman lost his challenge for Evander Holyfield's unified title in 1991, but his valiant performance convinced the doubters that he was still a force. "Boxing is just a sport. I wish I had this same attitude back then. I would have been heavyweight champion from 1974, to this day", claimed an older and wiser Foreman.

The first part of George Foreman's redemption was when he lost to Evander Holyfield in 1991 for the unified world heavyweight title. It was a hard fight, a moral victory for the hoary warrior. Foreman seemed determined to erase the image of the falling giant crashing dazed to the canvas from Muhammad Ali's punches in 1974. "I never look back. I live in the present. I barely remember the Seventies. If I try and look back it is like an old man looking back at his childhood", claimed Foreman.

He kept fighting, but an odd defeat in 1993 against Tommy Morrison in a vacant WBO fight appeared to end the comeback of the preacher. It was Foreman's 76th fight, his fourth decade of competition and he looked lost. "I need to get the anger back", he said, after returning to his pulpit at the Church of the Lord Jesus Christ, in the Aldine section of northeast Houston.

In the summer of 1994 promoter Bob Arum put together a fight between Michael Moorer and Foreman for the WBA and IBF titles. Moorer was at the time the man who beat the man who beat the man – James "Buster" Douglas knocked out Mike Tyson, Evander Holyfield ko'd Douglas and Moorer beat Holyfield.

The WBA initially refused to sanction the fight but Foreman had his day in court. The WBA walked away with $300,000 in sanctioning fees and Foreman with three million. On November 5, 1994, he had his night in the ring – the passage from George I to George II was complete. Big George was 45 and a grandfather.

▶ FOREMAN THE SHOWMAN

Before the fight with Michael Moorer veteran trainer, Angelo Dundee, adjusts the waistband on Foreman's red velvet shorts – the same shorts he wore when he beat Joe Frazier 21 years earlier. Foreman was the lightest he had been for six years. He trained twice each day: once in public, which was a comic performance, and once behind closed doors.

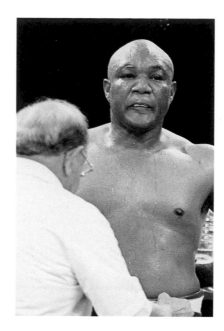

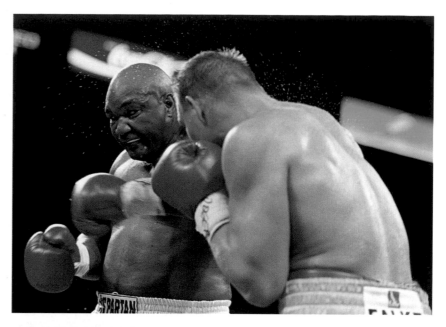

▲ FOREMAN V SCHULZ

In their 1995 fight Axel Schulz did enough to win, but the judges went with Foreman. "He was running and hiding" said Foreman after the verdict. "To beat me a man must fight. I will only retire after a true licking, not a boxing lesson."

◀ LOST ANGER NOT A PROBLEM

"The other Foreman was more interested in hurting people, the fame and the money. Not in that order – I think I liked the hurting more", said Foreman, who lost on points to Tommy Morrison (seen here landing a chilling right) in 1993.

"I want to punish him and knock him out cleanly" – Mike Tyson, 1991

For Tyson, life after Tokyo was difficult. He was out of control. In 1991 he beat Canada's Donovan "Razor" Ruddock twice, but both were hard, intensive struggles. The first fight ended in round seven and was followed by a brawl in the ring. Ruddock had refused to be intimidated and had caught and hurt Tyson, while his handlers thought that the referee, Richard Steele, was too quick with his stoppage. The rematch went 12.

A fight with Holyfield was planned but on July 19, 1991, Tyson changed his life forever when he raped an 18-year-old beauty contestant at the Canterbury Hotel in Indianapolis. The rape took place at 2 am and Tyson flew back to Cleveland that same morning. When he was arrested he could not even remember Desiree Washington's name.

Tyson was found guilty in February 1992. The trial lasted 17 days and when it was over he dropped his head and simply said "Oh, man." It was the end for him. He protested his innocence and before sentencing promised to change his life. "I have treated women bad, but that is all behind me. I will never return to that way of life", he stated before beginning his three year sentence.

Tyson was gone and nobody in the business of boxing missed him.

▼ **A LOOK OF DISDAIN**

Tyson stares at Ruddock as the Canadian tries to clamber up from the canvas in round seven of their first fight in 1991.

▶ NO PEACE FOR TYSON

"Before losing (to "Buster" Douglas) I had a great deal – I mean a big voracious appetite with women and stuff", said Tyson in 1990. "Now I look at womens' eyes and I see the devil." He never found a sanctuary from his urges and in 1991 raped Desiree Washington.

▲ TYSON BEHIND BARS

The American public make their feelings known, as they protest outside the courtroom. The case was a disaster for Tyson. In February 1992 he was found guilty of rape and sentenced to 10 years in prison, although he was given parole in March 1995. He still maintains his innocence.

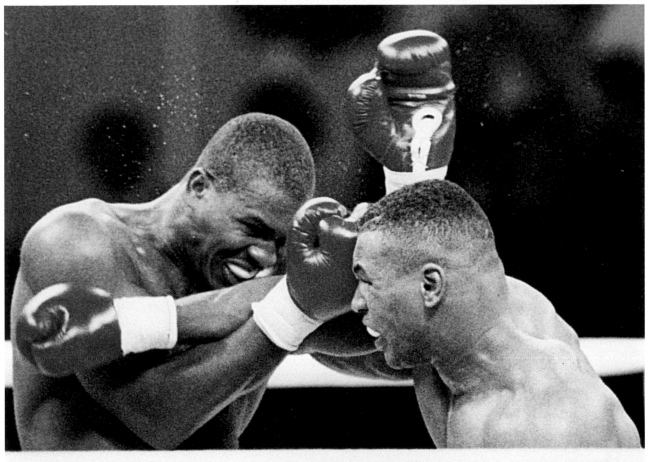

◀ UGLY SCENES RUIN WIN

Tyson on the ascendancy against Donovan "Razor" Ruddock on his way to victory in their first encounter. Regrettably, Tyson's celebrations were marred by an ugly brawl between the fighters' respective cornermen.

WILD DAYS

and

NIGHTS

Dark clouds loom for McCall as Bruno finally reaches his zenith

▲ **FOURTH TIME LUCKY!**

Bruno reaches out with yet another left jab, the punch which eventually wore down McCall and wrested the WBC belt from him. "The last round was the longest three minutes of my life", said Bruno after the fight. "I knew I just had to stay away and I would win." His finest hour was clouded by rumours of McCall's drug abuse, but nobody made their concerns public before the fight.

When Frank Bruno won the WBC title in 1995 it was the end of an unbelievable odyssey for a man blessed with brawn but cursed by distinct lack of fighting instincts. Bruno's persistent failing was his unfortunate knack of freezing and often dropping his guard when he was under sustained pressure. It was a weakness that had left him in a perilous state on four occasions, and had sabotaged all his previous title challenges. Against McCall, though, he finally earned his glory.

In a sport where negotiation is crucial, contacts essential, and talent merely preferable, Bruno and dozens of other champions like him have won world championships. In the awful reality of the business of boxing Bruno was as deserving as many and probably more deserving than most.

Elsewhere in the heavyweight world the mass confusion continued. The wild career of George Foreman, the WBU champion, rumbled on. He narrowly defeated Germany's Axel Schulz in early 1995, easily beat Crawford Grimsley in late 1996 and scraped past New Yorker, Lou Savarese, in 1997. He eventually quit the ring in November 1997, after a dubious points defeat to Shannon Briggs.

"I was never fast or nimble, I just knocked people out back then", Foreman said in Tokyo after Grimsley had run for 12 rounds. When asked about meeting Frazier and Ali in one of boxing's halcyon periods he replied: "I can't even remember that far back." Foreman, like fellow ring veteran Larry Holmes, was still fighting and making money in his late 40s.

▶ A TRUE BRITISH HERO

Bruno proudly parades his WBC belt in front of the press. A lifetime's ambition is realized for Bruno, after clinging on in the final round to complete a memorable victory.

▼ GLORY IS SHORT-LIVED

No one could deny Bruno his glory night in the ring against Oliver McCall, but he came unstuck in his very first defence against an explosive Tyson. "I don't think he (Tyson) has improved since 1989, and I know I have", said Bruno, but the contest was over in three rounds. Bruno had taken the most savage beating of his career and he never fought again.

MILESTONES OF BOXING

• • • • • • • • • • • • • • • • •

GOLDEN BOY BEATS THE OLD WARRIOR

The blood on Julio Cesar Chavez's face could not hide his bitter disappointment at the end of his WBC super-lightweight defence against Oscar De La Hoya, the perfumed Golden Boy from Los Angeles, in June 1996.

Chavez lost his title when the fight was stopped because of a wicked two-inch cut above his left eye in round four. The cut opened in the first minute of round one and Chavez claimed it happened five days before the fight in a late sparring session. At the time of the stoppage De La Hoya's speed and Chavez's disability had turned the long-awaited clash into a one-sided encounter between a brilliant young star and a faded master.

The angry reaction to Chavez's disclosure caused him to alter his story and claim the cut was actually done 25 days before the fight. It was Chavez's 100th fight and his 34th world title fight, but when it was over the former Mexican idol was in De La Hoya's shadow.

237

TYSON v HOLYFIELD

Holyfield's Ear was Left Ruined by a Beast

▼ ONE OFFENCE TOO MANY

A visibly distressed Evander Holyfield clutches his right ear in agony after Mike Tyson tore a chunk from it in round three of their rematch in June 1997. The missing piece of Holyfield's ear was later found on the canvas. In the days after the fight Holyfield was in forgiving mood: "The pressure was on him", said Holyfield. "He got hit with some good shots and he reacted. I know he is sorry, but he did it."

Within an hour of Tyson beating Seldon, the debacle was forgotten and the next encounter was already being hyped. At the post-fight press conference Seldon was replaced by Holyfield, who sat down next to King. Tyson was at the other end of the table, his now customary bored expression firmly in place.

As Don King jubilantly announced November 9, 1996, as the date of the fight, Tyson sneered, "I will have fun on the night." Holyfield smiled his smile and left the following morning for the fifth week of his 15-week-long stint at a Houston training camp. Tyson, meanwhile, went to a party. The alarm bells were already ringing.

Holyfield was the rank outsider, the underdog and in Las Vegas there was no indication that Tyson would lose. In the gym his sessions followed a predictable pattern. He hit a procession of static sparring partners and his entourage did the only thing they were required to do – they applauded.

But on the night Holyfield would not be intimidated. He had prayed to be protected from his own bravery and his belief was miraculous. Tyson unwisely made few, if any, concessions to his opponent's ability to find something from some dark place, and paid the price for his complacency.

In round six Tyson was over from a left hook. His body language altered and he started to lose. By round 10 the Holyfield miracle was nearly complete and Tyson, the bully, was saved by the bell. It ended in round 11 and Holyfield was champion for the third time. Tyson was already a blur in the shadows of his enormous entourage before judgement was passed and his diminished status conferred on him. "I lost to the better man", he bravely admitted.

King and his men, Horne and Holloway, were stunned and Tyson entered a muted trance. There was only one thing to do – a rematch. Nobody doubted Holyfield would agree and a date was set.

The so-called "Bite of the Century" took place on June 28, 1997, and came to be one of the sport's most degrading moments. It ended, in round three, when Tyson tore a chunk from the side of Holyfield's right ear and spat it out. Afterwards, he bit the left ear. It was the final act of shame for the brutal boy, whose money had seldom brought him peace of mind. He was belatedly disqualified by theatrical referee Mills Lane at the end of the round.

The fight's conclusion created hysteria in the crowd of 16,331 and there was later a stampede on the casino floor when people mistakenly believed they had heard gunshots. The MGM later withdrew from their one remaining fight with Don King.

"I don't know what happened that night. It's pretty embarrassing. That was just striking out in total hatred right there. I shouldn't have done that. Just for one moment I forgot that he was a human being", said Tyson three months after the fight. On the night Tyson and his manager Horne disgraced themselves when they made comments about Holyfield.

King and Tyson went missing after the fight – neither met the press. Meanwhile, Holyfield was at the hospital having 15 stitches inserted. Condemnation of Tyson's actions was unanimous and in July 1997 his licence to box was revoked by the Nevada State Commission. Although he can apply each year for a new licence, he will never get back the respect he once had and there are many who believe he should never be allowed to box again.

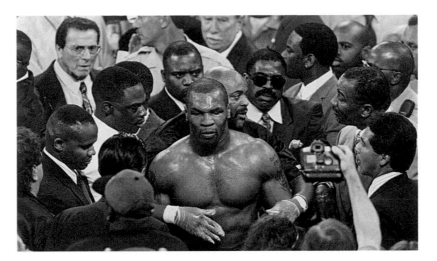

◄ **A LONELY WALK BACK**
Tyson is led away in disgrace after the shameful ear-biting episode. "I regret what I did. I want to apologize to Evander. He is a great champion and I made a mistake", said Tyson.

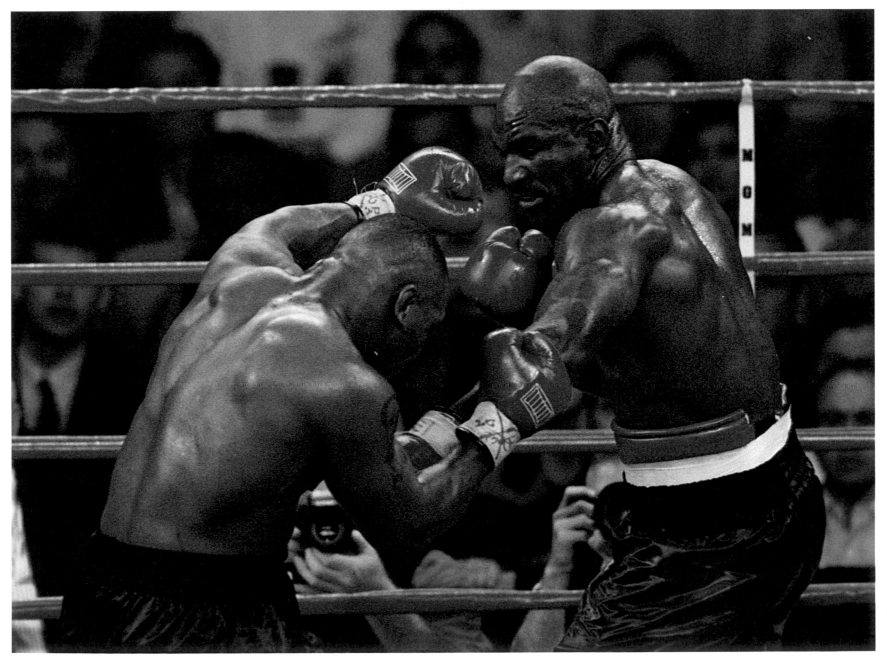

▲ **TYSON HUMBLED** *Holyfield pressurizes Tyson on his way to beating the champion in November 1996, in one of the shocks of the decade.*

Super-middleweights steal the show

▶ **BENN V COLLINS II**

*Steve Collins (right) launches an
assault on Nigel Benn in the second
of their two fights in 1996. The
fights attracted a total of over
40,000 people – a turn out which
emphasized the allure of the super-
middleweight divsion.*

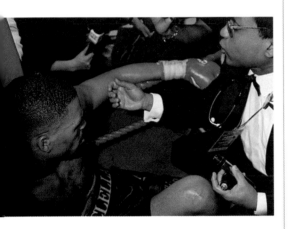

▲ **TRAGEDY STRIKES AGAIN**

*Gerald McClellan is slumped on
the floor in his corner while a
doctor examines him. The titanic
battle with Britain's Nigel Benn
had a tragic outcome for
McClellan. Benn was also taken
to hospital for observation.*

The British super-middleweights have created images
in fights that will never be forgotten. Their
performances turned a weight class that was at first
perceived as an oddity, into arguably the second most
lucrative division in boxing.

In 1995 Nigel Benn defended his WBC version
when he survived two knockdowns and a terrible
beating to stop former middleweight champion
Gerald McClellan, a fighter with a fearsome
reputation as a puncher in America. The fight's
dramatic end in round 10 was overshadowed by news
that McClellan later required emergency surgery to
remove a blood clot from his brain. He survived, but
he remains blind and deaf.

Also in 1995, over 50,000 people watched Dublin's

Steve Collins, who started his career in Boston as an
apprentice in the same gym as Marvin Hagler, beat
Chris Eubank twice in the Republic of Ireland.

The following year, Collins, the WBO champion,
also beat Benn twice. Both fights were in Manchester
and were attended by nearly 22,000 on each
occasion. Eubank, Benn and Collins are part of British
and Irish sporting history.

Also that year, Robin Reid, who won a bronze
medal for Britain at the Barcelona Olympics in 1992,
won the WBC version in Italy.

In 1997 Collins retired because a fight with Roy
Jones could not be made. His vacant WBO title was
won by Joe Calzaghe, an unbeaten fighter from
Wales, who narrowly outpointed Eubank.

MILESTONES OF BOXING

• • • • • • • • • • • • • • • • •

THE BITE OF THE CENTURY

The unforgivable act of a beast scarred Evander Holyfield and boxing forever on a hot June night in 1997. Mike Tyson chewed off part of Holyfield's ear and admitted his act was senseless.

In July 1997, Tyson was fined three million dollars and his licence to fight was revoked by the Nevada State Athletic Commission. Tyson can apply each July for a new licence.

"Tyson is not finished as a boxer", said Luther Mack, one of the commissioners after the hearing in Las Vegas which Tyson chose not to attend. Two months later he missed a reconciliation meeting between himself and Holyfield, that Muhammad Ali had organized in Louisville. He claimed that his private jet had broken down on the runway.

"I will not fight the punishment. I will learn from this horrible mistake", said Tyson. In the months after the fight Tyson vanished; there were rumours of wayward behaviour and he hinted that there was a chance he would never fight again.

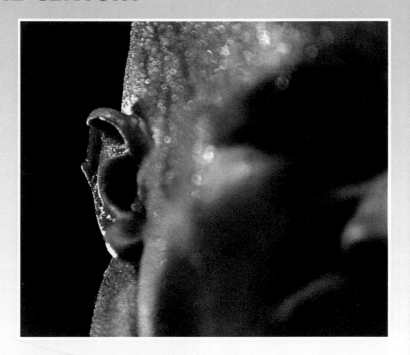

◄ **THE CELTIC WARRIOR**
Chris Eubank had remained undefeated for 43 fights before he lost his WBO super-middleweight belt to courageous Irishman, Steve Collins, in March 1995. The pair fought again in September the same year, but the outcome was the same. "There is nothing I can do, he is just too strong", Eubank complained to his trainer during the rematch. Eubank quit the sport, but he returned in 1996.

Golden Boy fights Macho Man in front of adoring fans in Vegas

Where will it all end? The somewhat farcical senior tour of boxers sunk to new depths in 1997, when Sugar Ray Leonard was stopped in five rounds by the slightly less ancient Hector "Macho" Camacho. Leonard was 40, Camacho 34. In 1996 Camacho had outpointed Roberto Duran.

Camacho's wild spree as boxing's resident lunatic started in the early 1980s when he first won a world title. In 1991, he was arrested for driving with his girlfriend on his lap. "I was doing the vehicular wild thing" he explained.

After beating Leonard, a fight was made between the "Macho Man" and Oscar De La Hoya, who in 1997 hired and then fired, Emanuel Steward. Like many of Camacho's fights it was a dull affair – his fights were seldom equal to his hype. "I came to win and I fought a damn courageous fight", claimed Camacho. In truth, he held and ran, and was at his annoying best.

The fight served two purposes: it gave a clear indication of how good De La Hoya was, whilst demonstrating just how far back Leonard, Duran, Camacho and the rest of the relics had gone.

De La Hoya had won the WBC welterweight title in early 1997 from Pernell Whitaker in a technical fight that ended with a controversial decision. Whitaker wanted a rematch but Bob Arum, De La Hoya's promoter, refused.

Although wonderfully gifted fighters, Roy Jones and Oscar De La Hoya lacked a certain something, but the third boxer from the time, Naseem Hamed, had the look. He walked the walk and talked the talk. He was a different type of champion – he had a sharp mouth to accompany his fearsome fists.

◀ **BAD BOY UNDER THE GLOSS**

"He (De La Hoya) has an image. He looks like a choir boy, talks nice and sweet and then in the gym and the ring he changes. He transforms into one of the most cold-blooded killers I've ever seen" , said Emanuel Steward shortly before the Camacho fight.

▲ **ONE OF THE GREATS**

Oscar De La Hoya celebrates his victory over Hector Camacho. "I beat Chavez and Whitaker and they were the best pound-for-pound fighters in the world. It is me now", stated the Golden Boy. However against Camacho and Whitaker there were worrying signs that his power was missing.

▶ **STEWARD OUT THE DOOR**

De La Hoya is held aloft by members of his entourage after defeating Camacho – however there was tension in the camp. Shortly after the fight De La Hoya split from Emanuel Steward, his trainer of only a few months. There were several rumours, all denied, that Steward was trying to get De La Hoya to leave promoter, Bob Arum, and join Don King.

245

Butterbean and Martin prove surprise attractions in the 1990s

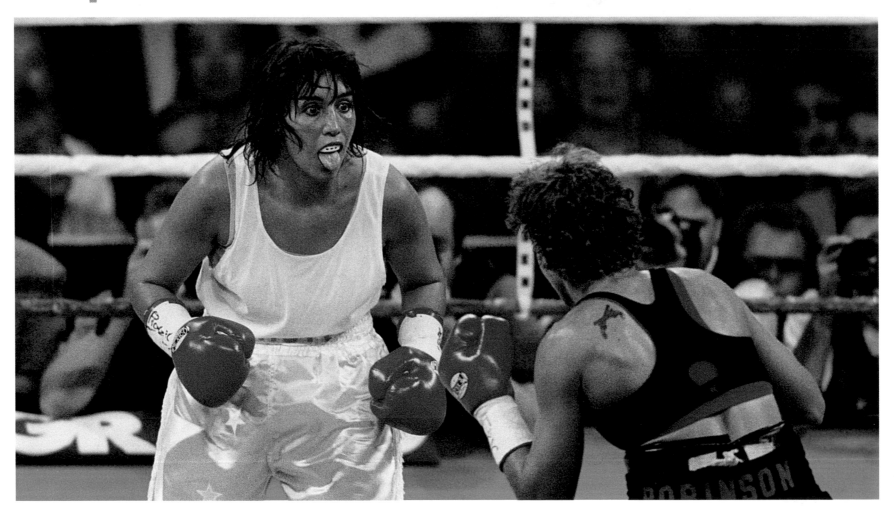

Butterbean is just one of modern boxing's eccentric acts. Christy Martin, the coal miner's daughter, is another. Both have made more money than ordinary boxers at their weight.

In the early 1990s Butterbean, or Eric Esch, was a construction worker in Alabama, but by the mid-1990s he was the undisputed king of flab and the IBA, one of 12 sanctioning bodies, gave him their super-heavyweight four-round championship title. It is the world's least significant belt and has to be a full 60 inches long to go round Butterbean's gut.

"I have the urge to win just like I have the urge to eat ice cream" claims Butterbean. The fans love the freak show and because he has so few skills he is seldom in a dull fight.

Christy Martin is the best known of the female boxers to emerge in the 1990s. She is a natural fighter, not a natural boxer, and has gained her fame on the undercard of Don King's shows. Critics claim that she has ignored other women, many of whom were former kick boxers from Europe, who fought for women's world titles.

Both Martin and Butterbean provide new boxing fans with some quality entertainment, but whereas Butterbean's talents are crude and limited, Martin and her fellow fighters are being afforded greater credibility. Women's boxing has existed since the 1920s, but Martin has brought it to the forefront. As women continue to expand and develop their skills the fan base will undoubtedly grow.

▲ **MARTIN TAUNTS ROBINSON**
Christy Martin easily defeats Melinder Robinson (above) in four rounds in July 1996. "I fight for Christy Martin", she explains, "I'm not at the front of any revolution."

▶ **A HUG FOR THE BEAN**

"I'm the best four-round fighter in the world", says Butterbean, who is pictured here after beating George Clarke in one round. At 322 pounds he is undeniably a high-profile attraction.

▲ **NOT RUNNING SCARED**

" If they run I can still catch them", explains Butterbean. At the super-heavyweight end of the business credibility is a distant notion with no real meaning.

MILESTONES OF BOXING

• • • • • • • • • • • • • •

THE END OF THE ANCIENT DAYS

Big George Foreman quit the ring in 1977 after losing to Jimmy Young and in November 1997 he quit again after a dubious points loss to New York's Shannon Briggs.

Foreman was six weeks shy of his 49th birthday and taking part in his 81st fight. He was the missing link in boxing's journey from the past to its future.

His fight with Shannon Briggs was for the "linear" championship – it was the title Foreman kept after the WBA and IBF stripped him, and after he decided to relinquish the WBU version.

"I have not lost since knocking out Michael Moorer in 1994", he said before losing to Briggs. After his victory, Briggs became the unlikely recipient of the linear championship, while Foreman was left to reflect: "I'm done. I'm going home, it has been a great ride", he said.

New stars are poised to take boxing into the next Millennium

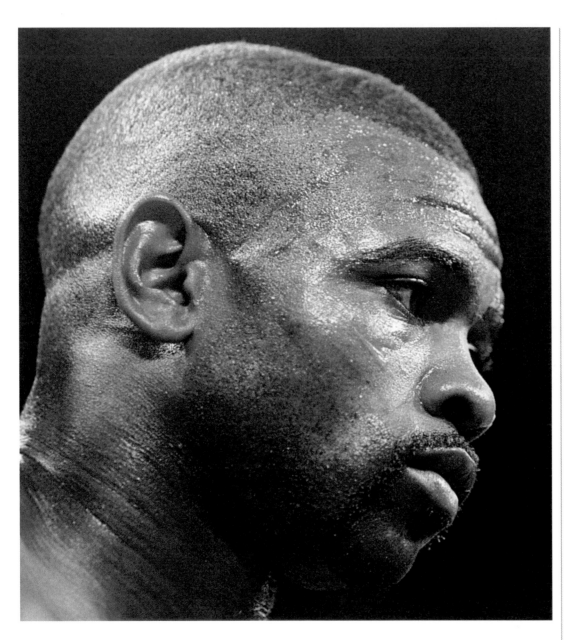

▲ **A NEW HEAVYWEIGHT**

In late 1997 Roy Jones decided to step up to join the ranks of the heavyweights, but refused fights with both WBO champion, Herbie Hide, and James "Buster" Douglas, leading to speculation over his future intents.

The news that Roy Jones may join the heavyweights put a bizarre seal on 1997. It was a year that started with the tears of Oliver McCall, and also included the maiming of Evander Holyfield's ear. There seemed no end in sight to the amazing scenes at the top of the sport's mad realm, and there was also little hope of a heavyweight unification fight when negotiations broke down between Holyfield and Lewis.

Elsewhere some great potential fights vanished. The loss suffered by Terry Norris in a supposedly routine WBC light-middleweight title defense, against Keith Mullings, ruined a planned showdown with Oscar De La Hoya. However, WBC welterweight champion De La Hoya only has to look across at WBA champion, Ike "Bazooka" Quartey, or the IBF's Felix Trinidad for a potential unification fight.

There is a chance for one of these fighters to attain greatness in the welterweight division, but he will have to be willing to prove himself against the other champions. De La Hoya has the opportunity. At featherweight, Hamed has fewer options but a move through the weight divisions could produce some of the fights of the decade.

Jones had relinquished the middle, super-middle and light-heavyweight titles in his pursuit of excellence. He could have met Dublin's Steve Collins in late 1997 but both parties wanted too much money. Collins opted to vacate his WBO super-middleweight title when he refused to fight Joe Calzaghe, who beat Chris Eubank for the belt. Calzaghe is just one fighter for the Millennium. There are dozens of others.

Ricardo Lopez ended 1997 as WBC strawweight champion and boasted an unbeaten record of 46 fights. He is a brilliant operator at the bottom of a pile of fighters in a sport dominated by excessive personalities. It has been the same since fists and gloves were first used. If Lopez, and not Jones, could move to heavyweight there would certainly be some fun. A fairy tale, once upon a distant fight: Lopez v Tyson for New Year's Eve 1999!

◀ **HOLYFIELD MUST WAIT**

After two stunning wins against Mike Tyson the only man left in the heavyweight division for Holyfield to fight was Lennox Lewis. However, initial negotiations broke down and the fight now looks unlikely to take place until at least the end of 1998.

▼ **JONES LANDS A LEFT**

Roy Jones (left) easily beat James Toney when they met in Las Vegas in 1994. The victory helped establish Jones as one of the finest fighters in the world.

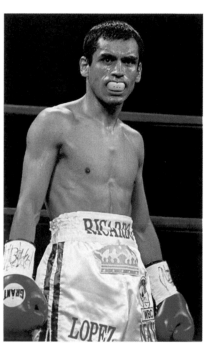

▲ **A MEXICAN IDOL**

Ricardo Lopez is the forgotten man of boxing, but at the start of 1998 he was undefeated in 46 fights and held both the WBO and WBC strawweight titles. Many consider him to be the best pound-for-pound fighter in the world.